Claire McGowan is the author of multiple novels in both the crime and women's fiction genres. She also writes for radio and TV, as well as being a popular teacher of creative writing. She grew up in a small village in Ireland, which much like Mr Darcy she did find rather confined and unvarying.

Sarah Day's debut novel, *Mussolini's Island*, received a 2018 Betty Trask Award and was shortlisted for the Polari First Book Prize and the Historical Writers' Association Debut Crown. With a background in science communication, she has worked as a press officer, magazine editor and freelance writer, and was Writer in Residence at Gladstone's Library in 2019. She lives in London.

Pride and Prejudice on Social Media

Sarah Day and Claire McGowan

HODDERstudio

First published in Great Britain in 2021 by Hodder Studio
An Imprint of Hodder & Stoughton Ltd
An Hachette UK company

1

Photography by Johnny Ring © Hodder & Stoughton
Other photographs © Shutterstock

A CIP catalogue record for this title is available from the British Library

Hardback ISBN 9781529370164

Typeset by Hewer Text UK Ltd, Edinburgh
Printed and bound in Great Britain by Clays Ltd, Elcograf S.p.A.

Hodder & Stoughton policy is to use papers that are natural, renewable
and recyclable products and made from wood grown in sustainable
forests. The logging and manufacturing processes are expected to
conform to the environmental regulations of the country of origin.

Hodder & Stoughton Ltd
Carmelite House
50 Victoria Embankment
London EC4Y 0DZ

www.hodder.co.uk

*Pride and Prejudice
on Social Media*

Introduction

Greetings, gentlefolk!

The document you are about to peruse came into my possession via a circuitous route, of which gentle lips dare not speak. Suffice it to say, it is a chronicle of Hertfordshire society and of a family cursed with five daughters and a property entailed away from the female line. #womensrightsnow

Thrown into uproar by the arrival in their small social sphere of not one, but two eligible SMLFs (single man, large fortune), the Bennet sisters must flirt, fight and overcome their own pride, and indeed prejudice (you see where I'm going with this), to secure their good fortunes.

The following messages have been 'hacked' from the telephonic devices of the various actors in our drama and, via their private correspondences, offer a glimpse of the ups and downs, twists and turns, reversals and surprises that pave the way to the altar. (Spoiler alert.)

Your correspondent,

xoxo J. Austen

Dramatis Personae

The Bennet Family

Jane Bennet
@JaneBennet

beautiful, sweet and generous, but unfortunately penniless

Elizabeth/Lizzy Bennet
@pertopinionsfineeyes @excellentwalker

arch, witty, pretty, but also sadly penniless

Mary Bennet
@ProudBluestocking

all about those rewards of sober reflection

Kitty Bennet
@KittyCatB

in the shadow of her sisters. Prone to giggling and profligate coughing

Lydia Bennet
@LydiaBennet

not shy in coming forward. A determined flirt despite being the youngest of all the Bennet sisters

Mr Bennet
@mrbennet

long-suffering king of the sarcastic put-down

Mrs Bennet
@mrsbennet

she may be a little extra, but someone has to get these five girls married off . . .

The Bingleys and the Darcys

Charles Bingley
@abingleybingbong

single man, large fortune, happy manners – says it all, really

Caroline Bingley
@carolineinthecity

his sister. Her tongue is as sharp as her head-feathers are high. Determined to make herself Mrs Darcy at the earliest opportunity

Louisa Hurst
@easylouisa

Charles's older, married sister. Plays extremely rapidly upon the pianoforte. Yes, she is judging your dress and decorum

Mr Hurst
Louisa's husband. Loves port, sport, cards, a cheeky snooze on the chaise and nothing else

Fitzwilliam Darcy
@puttingonthefitz @derbyshirelad

Charles's BFF. Po-faced yet devastatingly handsome and absolutely minted. Not skilled at first impressions

Georgiana Darcy
@georgianadarcy

his sister. Sweet and shy. Not sufficiently cad-resistant

Colonel Fitzwilliam
the Darcys' cousin. Younger son of an earl and therefore tragically only partially well off

Lady Catherine de Bourgh
@herladyship

the Darcys' aunt. Terrifying and rich. Noble patroness of Mr Collins

Other characters

George Wickham
@keptfromthepulpit

handsome and charming redcoat, hiding a terrible secret (or several)

Colonel Forster, Denny, Carter
the Hertfordshire militia, aka Redcoats on Tour.

Mr and Mrs Gardiner
uncle and aunt to the Bennet girls, residing in London

Mr and Mrs Philips
uncle and aunt to the Bennet girls, residing in nearby Meryton

Sir William and Lady Lucas
their recent ennoblement does not negate a lowly background in trade. On a rival mission to marry off several daughters of limited means

Charlotte Lucas
@CharlotteLucas

their eldest daughter and Elizabeth's BFF. Tragic spinster of 27

Maria Lucas
@marialikecareylucas

her terrified younger sister

William Collins
@thefunvicar

cousin to Mr Bennet and future beneficiary of the Bennet estate, thanks to the patriarchy. Suitor to Lizzy/Charlotte (anyone will do, really)

Hill and Sarah
long-suffering servants to the Bennet family at Longbourn

Nicholls
servant to the Bingley family at Netherfield Park. Makes a mean white soup

@NapoleonBonerPart
mysterious online troll and notorious cad. Tradesmen, lock up your daughters

AskJane

Logged in: Charles Bingley

SEARCH HISTORY

🔍 Rental property 3 billiard rooms plus

Hertfordshire rental enough rooms to avoid sister

Dance scene Hertfordshire

Meryton Community Discussion Forum
Confined and unvarying since 1653

15 August 1811

Houses to let in the area
Latest Posts
Posted by **Capital Relocation**

Netherfield Park is available to let. 3br (billiard rooms), 16 servants, space for several uninvited house guests and a small ball of 200–300 people. Would suit a single young man of fortune looking for a starter mansion.

Possible French sightings
Latest Posts
Posted by **unwedmaiden23**

Just a heads-up, saw someone hanging around the high street bonnet shop, could have been French, pretty sure he was hiding a baguette, stay safe people.

Recycling news
Latest Posts
Posted by **Meryton District Council**

The rag and bone men come on Thursdays now. Please use the blue basket and do not mix up your rags and your bones!!! Very important.

Comment /asimpleesquire someone left their rags in my bone box last week, pls remove before collection day is upon us.

Free exchange
Latest Posts
Posted by **dashwood123**

Three servants, no longer needed but in good condition. Some wear and tear consistent with normal use. Getting rid due to sudden reversal of fortunes on death of father. Collection only.

Lonely hearts
Latest Posts

Posted by **missnotmrs**

Unmarried spinster, 25 but mostly own teeth, mild signs of
consumption, seeks bachelor with 1,000 a year ONO. Widowers
accepted. No cads or time wasters.

Lost and found
Latest Posts

Posted by **Meryton Assembly Rooms**

Found: one corset after last Assembly Rooms dance, name 'Lydia'
sewn inside.

Plague news – how to stay compliant
Latest Posts

Posted by **Public Health Hertfordshire**

Reminder that the plague is spreading in Hertfordshire. You must stay
one swords-width/two pigs-width apart, wash your hands at least once
a week, and shield your face with a veil or very long feather when
visiting the bonnet shop or a sickly poor person for charitable good
works.

Comment **/conspiracytheorist** This is ridiculous, there is no plague
in Meryton and it's totally unfair we should be rated as Sphere 2 when
Bedfordshire is Sphere 1.

Comment **/swordoftruth** There is no plague anyway it's a French
conspiracy! Designed to boost the sales of face veils!

Comment **/smileysarah** All you need to do is suck a lemon,
everyone knows that

> **Reply by /lemons4less** I have two lemons for sale £1000 each
> no time wasters

15 September 1811

Charles
Hey kinsfolk! And **@Fitzwilliam** my BFF
(best Fitz forevaaa, lol!). Thinking about
renting a small mansion for the autumn
or longer. Bit sick of moving about
between different AirHosteleries.
What about Netherfield Park in
Hertfordshire? **https://capitalreloca-
tion.com/NetherfieldPark** It has
three billiard rooms which is really the
bare minimum tbh

Caroline
Urgh not another rental, Charles! When
will you get on the property footstool?

Charles
No rush! Love møving about! Next
gen can sort that out LOL

Fitzwilliam
Outside of London? What about
the society though?

Charles
Country manners? Love 'em, mate!
♥

Fitzwilliam
Just seen the name of this group.
Caroline, was this you? Change it
please

Caroline
What about Bingley-Darcy? Has a
nice ring to it 😏

Fitzwilliam
What?

Caroline
Nothing. House looks decent
enough to me, Charles bro, as long
as you've got your favourite sister
to keep house for you . . . 😊

Louisa
Joint favourite! Me and Hubs will
visit of course, won't we
@MrHurst?

Mr Hurst
Will there be any sport?

Remember the rules of the group!
– When your daughters are all wed you must leave the group
– Do not corset-block in favour of your own daughters at balls
– No gloating if you manage to marry off your daughters
– No promoting of goods or services (Karen, no one cares about your online bonnet shop)
– No hate speech (except against the French)

Glossary:
ID – impoverished daughter
TTW – trying to wed
SMLF – single man, large fortune
EE – entailed estate
SH – sarcastic husband
BAE – bachelor approaching engagement

Posted by **Lady Lucas** 20 September 1811
OMG Meryton ladies, Netherfield Park is let at last! A Mr Bingley from the North. Apparently handsome and agreeable. And best of all he is a SMLF!!! 👀
#2 IDs #10yearsTTW

Comment by /Mrs Bennet Wow! How much?
#5IDs #5yearsTTW #oneEE #oneSH

> **Reply by /Lady Lucas** Five thousand a year. Found his profile:
> **www.singlemanlargefortune.com/charlesbingleyesq**

> > **Reply by /Mrs Bennet** ❤️👰 Maybe he will marry your Charlotte, so sad to see her an old maid at 27

Reply by /Lady Lucas You're too kind Mrs B. But with five unwed daughters you should really be looking to your own troubles 😬

Reply by /Mrs Bennet Well you know people do say Jane is the hottest girl for five counties. Don't like to boast about my own daughter, but that's what they say!

Reply by /Mrs Long I heard he was bringing 12 ladies with him tho so don't get excited

This post has been flagged as misinformation or fake news

Charles Bingley @abingleybingbong

27 SEPTEMBER 1811

Moving day!! Excited to start a new chapter by moving to Hertfordshire and Netherfield Park . . . So stressful when you have a mansion to furnish and only five landaus but thankfully I have excellent staff!! #ThanksButlers #TipYourHousemaids #Aristolife #LOL (landauing out loud!!) #yolo (you only landau once)

@NapoleonBonerPart I'd like to come over and tip your housemaids know what I mean

Good Day!

EXCLUSIVE PICTURES: Caroline Bingley invites us into Netherfield Park, TELLS ALL on keeping house for her brother and how she's coped with an unexpected move to the countryside: 'I've stocked up on walking petticoats'.

Bye, babe! How to cope when a casual acquaintance ends up staying at your house for weeks

Oh brother! Directing clueless relatives to marry suitable well-connected girls

Get the guy: show off your figure with a turn about the room

Boy bye! Witty put-downs for any situation

50 top headdresses for under a guinea

30 September 1811

Lydia
Anyone seen my blue corset?

Mary
My morning piano recital starting in 10 minutes, please assemble in the drawing room

Kitty
Washing my hair!

Lydia
LOL no thanks

Jane
Mary, I have the soup kitchen at 12 but I can make it if you promise it's under three hours this time

Mrs Bennet
Never mind all that. Girls I have news! EVERYONE STAY CALM!!! A SMLF has just moved into Netherfield Park! All we need is for your dad to call on him and then he'll definitely marry one of you. Here's his profile: **www.singleman-largefortune.com/charlesbingl-eyesq** We have to move fast or Lady Lucas will be on it like a bonnet

Mr Bennet
And yet I am unmoved

Mrs Bennet
Oh that's just great, get ready to all die old maids thanks to your father

Lizzy
For a single man in possession of a good fortune must be in want of a wife!

Mrs Bennet
Oh we've got a comedian here. See how you like it when your father dies and you're out on the street. They don't let girls inherit houses you know! #sexist

Mr Bennet
Let us flatter ourselves, my dear, I might survive you!

Lizzy
Jesus Dad, not helpful

Jane
Mum's just trying to be nice. Personally I love meeting new people! Am sure they will all be lovely

Lydia
Meh. No redcoat no interest.

Kitty
THIS 😂

Mary
I find the rewards of sober reflection much more appealing – I should infinitely prefer a book #amreading

Mrs Bennet
Can everyone at least update their dating profiles wherever you have them?

Lizzy
Not Spinder, Lydia, we want marriages, not scandalous flirtations! Where IS your corset btw??

Mrs Bennet
It's all going to Puff-Guts Collins when your dad pegs it so if you're not married by then you'll be out on the lanes

Mr Bennet
Can we please give Cousin William his proper name?

Lydia
PUFF-GUTS!! PMSL

AskJane

Logged in: Mrs Bennet

SEARCH HISTORY

What is an entail

Q Can someone be arrested for inheriting an entailed property

How to marry off five daughters before husband carks it

Flutterings and tremors nerves

Lizzy Bennet
@pertopinionsfineeyes
Bio: Second of five daughters.
Likes walking, winking and
witticisms. She/Her

Lizzy Bennet @pertopinionsfineeyes
30th September 1811

The latest in an ongoing series: 'Stuff my
parents say'

Mum: Quick girls, a single man's moved into
the neighbourhood, maybe he'll marry you

Dad: Is that his design in moving here?
Careful if you go visit, he may like you best of
all!

Mum: 😕

 @NapoleonBonerPart your mum is a total
MILF (matron I'd like to forget) LOLLLLL

Myeligibleacquaintance.com

Jane, 22

Jane is the eldest of five sisters, and five times as pretty as the rest of us! She also has the sweetest disposition. Be warned, our family's estate is entailed away from the female line so she must take care to marry a man of good fortune. (#jokes #butnotreally)

Verywellcupid.com

Lizzy, 20

Loves: walking, lively conversation and happy manners. Hates: proud disagreeable men, bores, men out of their wits. Perfect date: a long, muddy walk. Please, no poetry. I wonder who first discovered how effective it is in driving away love.

Tweeharmony.com

Mary, 19

Mother made me build this page. I find the benefits of observation and reflection to be much greater than those of dancing, travel or trivial conversation. Hobbies: reading great books and making extracts. *Fordyce's Sermons* 4life.

Marrymyimpoverisheddaughter.com

Kitty, 17

Loves redcoats, giggling and living in the shadow of my FOUR sisters (groan). Add me on Snapbavardage!! Pls no breeches etchings or French people.

Spinder.com – hot spinsters in your area!

Lydia, 15

See you on the dance floor. Or maybe I'll call on you early before you are dressed, ummmm! Swipe right on my etchings if you're a redcoat.

OCT

18

1811

Meryton Town Dance

Host - Meryton District Council
6pm–11pm
Meryton Assembly Rooms

Join us for an evening of dancing and harmless social engagement.
Premium tickets include an exclusive meet and greet with newcomer to
the area Charles Bingley (SMLF), who will be attending with his two
sisters and entourage! (Entourage tbc.) This event is certified 'plague
safe', so please stay one swords-width apart and use your fan to shield
your face at all times.

Lydia Bennet
Gonna get lit tonite! Bring on da redcoats!

Sir William Lucas
Capital, capital! Dancing is one of the first refinements of
polished society

Fitzwilliam Darcy
And less polished ones. Any savage can dance.

Sir William Lucas

Caroline Bingley

 Mr Hurst
Will there be any port?

18 October 1811

Lizzy
Hey Charlotte, are you here yet? Please say you're here, am an absolute wallflower. Need BFF to snark in the corner with . . .

Charlotte
By the punch!

Phew. What do we think of the new guy?

Seems nice! He's dancing with Jane AGAIN! They've really hit it off – major #vibes

I know! Did someone light a fire because it's suddenly HAWT in here. Love this for her – she has liked many a stupider person. Looks like it's just you and me on the spinster bench.

Err alright for you, you're not even 1 and 20 mate. I'm 27!!!! Practically in the convent

Aww don't be ridiculous, you're a total catch. Who's Bingley brought with him? Maybe something there? ;)

Two sisters and a brother-in-law. Check out those head feathers, good LORD. And a mate.

What do we know about the mate? Just out of interest

Word on the lane is he's Mr Fitzwilliam Darcy, 10,000 a year

Oh interesting. Just me or is he kind of hot, in a grumpy way? Real tall, dark and handsome vibe mmmm

Honey everyone is hot on 10k a year. You should get Jane to intro you ASAP. Better to show more interest than you feel IMO. The menz are easily confused

Urgh you know me, not keen to marry unless real deep affection ya know?

Deep indeed 😜

Oh God they're heading this way. Quick – phones in reticules

18 October 1811

Fitzwilliam
Charles. Charles! FFS stop flirting and help me out here. Pretty sure she heard me say that

Charles
Chill out, mate, I'm sure she didn't hear you!

What did I say again? Not that bad, was it?

You said she was tolerable but not handsome enough to tempt you to dance

In my defence, I never dance

In her defence, she is quite hot

Maybe she heard but didn't know I was talking about her?

I literally said, oh look, that's Elizabeth Bennet over there, you should ask her to dance

That's . . . not good

It's fine, just stop thinking about it and come and have some white soup

She just walked past me and made a face

What sort of face?

Did . . . did you do that just now?

Why, do you think she looks a bit mad?

I think you look a bit mad tbh. Stop making etchings of women at balls

OK, she's looking. Stop texting. Meet you by the white soup

What is that? Is it a marrow? Why a marrow? Charles, I am having a situation here

AskJane

Logged in: Lizzy Bennet

SEARCH HISTORY

How to appear unbothered when handsome rich man calls you tolerable

Women who've got married after the age of 21 examples

Mr Darcy Pemberley landowner hot rich

18 October 1811

Jane
Maybe he didn't say 'tolerable'?
Maybe it was . . . knowledgeable

Lizzy
Is that better??

Forageable

Oh god

Anyway, he seems pretty awful so
it really doesn't matter. Hasn't
danced with anyone except
Bingley's sisters all night!

Soluble

Please stop saying words

18 October 1811

Mrs Bennet
OMG Mr B, what a night we're having. Jane is so admired!

Jane

Mrs Bennet
And Mr Bingley's sisters, so elegant! The lace on Mrs Hurst's gown, OMG!

Mrs Bennet
Mr B? Are you up? Mr Bingley's danced with Jane twice! Twice!! Started out with Charlotte Lucas though #rude

Lydia
Me and Kitty partnered for every dance so far! #fagged

Kitty
Mary busy being a wallflower obvs LOL

Mary
Like I ALREADY SAID, I should infinitely prefer a book. Balls hold no interest for me

Mr Bennet
Muting this chat now

Lizzy
Personally I think sisters seem up themselves! I heard one asking where the langoustines were on the buffet, like hello this is Hertfordshire not Paris

Mrs Bennet
And as for that Mr Darcy – he may be handsome but he slighted our Lizzy, said she was a troll

Lizzy
Um not exactly Mum

Mrs Bennet
Another time Lizzy I'd refuse to dance with him, see how he likes it then!

Lizzy
LOL – safe to say I will never dance with Mr Darcy!

18 October 1811

Caroline
God, what an insufferable evening. Stupid provincial people and the band didn't even know 'thank u next'. No langoustines on the buffet wtf

Mr Hurst
Port wasn't up to much. Only drank fourteen glasses

Louisa
lol babe, ur so funny 😄

Caroline
I heard Lizzy Bennet described as a reputed beauty but her engraving must be daguerreotypeshopped, what do you say **@Fitzwilliam**?

Fitzwilliam
I should as soon call her mother a wit

Caroline

Fitzwilliam
Why do you ask anyway? I hardly noticed her

Fitzwilliam
· Never mind, it doesn't matter

Charles
Well I never met with such hot ladies or fun times! You just need a positive mental outlook, Fitzwilliam – Have you tried that vision board etching kit I got you for Yuletide?

Fitzwilliam
Jesu Christ

18 October 1811

> **Fitzwilliam**
> What is your sister's deal? Why does she care what I think about Lizzy Bennet? Can't even remember what she looks like tbh

Charles
You might as well give in, Fitzwilliam, Caroline always gets what she wants in the end! The sound of wedding bells is deafening 🔔💒 Should I start calling you brother now or . . .?

> Look, it's not funny. Caroline's a lovely girl obvs but . . .

> Do you know if she said anything about it? Lizzy Bennet, that is. You know, what I said

Thought you didn't care?

Lizzy Bennet
@pertopinionsfineeyes
Bio: Second of five daughters.
Likes walking, winking and
witticisms. She/Her

Lizzy Bennet @pertopinionsfineeyes
19 October 1811

Stuff my sisters say:

Sister 1: OMG BAE is so agreeable, good-
humoured much ease love his happy manners
OMG
Me: Handsome too which really he ought to
be if poss
Sister 1: 💀
Me: The money doesn't hurt either

 @EmpireFirst
Typical femi-napoleon
 @NapoleonBonerPart
You left out one REALLY BIG thing a man
ought to have ;) 🍆

 @pertopinionsfineeyes
Ew why are men

Am I the Addlepate?

AITA for not dancing even though gentlemen were scarce?

Posted by **derbyshirelad** 20 October 1811

In the title really. My friend (22M) really likes dancing and I (27M) am staying with him for a spell. Not really ready to be on my own just now due to What Happened (post for another day). Anyway, he's great, but he ALWAYS wants to go out. I'd rather stay in with a good book. I really hate dancing, so I mostly just hang out in the corner and watch people (not in a creepy way). He's always going on about how I should be dancing and pointing out women he dares say might be very agreeable and I'm just not into it. If they're so great, why isn't someone already dancing with them? There was this one woman (not sure of age, quite old – like 20, I'd guess) he wouldn't stop going on about so in the end I said she wasn't handsome enough to dance with and I'm afraid she may have overheard. AWKWARD.

Also, does anyone know what this means?

TL;DR I hate dancing but my friend wants me to dance all the time
AITA

Comment /hertfordshireruuuuuules NTA. Your friend sounds like a total douche, you're awesome for messing with him

Comment /independentspinster Errr OP you've kind of buried the lede here. What about this woman overhearing you saying she's not fit enough, that's not cool. YTA

Reply by /handlemyballs Her problem, she shouldn't be listening in on private conversations between guys. Also needs to sort out her appearance if it's causing her problems at balls and stuff NTA

> **Reply by /ladnotcad** Totally, classic femi-napoleon behaviour here, at a ball looking for guys' approval but can't take the truth

Comment /toffwhoboffs Check out my ThouTube channel /ballgames! Loads of stuff about how to pull ladies at balls e.g. tell them their corset makes them look fat IT WORKS

> **Reply by /sirhumpmedaily** All about the chemistry, amirite?

Comment /NapoleonBonerPart Surprised you can dance at all with that big ol stick up your bum
This post has been flagged for abuse

Thoughts from a proud bluestocking

Mary Bennet lives in Hertfordshire and believes a woman's reputation is no less brittle than it is beautiful. She enjoys playing concertos, reading sermons and despairing of her four sisters.

TOO MANY BALLS IN THE AIR

Some thoughts on dancing and our behaviour towards the undeserving of the other sex

23 October 1811

Balls balls balls. I'm absolutely drowning in balls. Tedious, unsanitary, sweaty, smelly balls. For those who feel similarly sullied, I've drafted some helpful tips for coping with your own struggles with men and their balls . . . First, place yourself at the pianoforte with some low-key funeral hymns . . .

Read more (73 pages, 7 candle read)

Drinks at Lucas Lodge

Host - Sir William Lucas
5pm–late
Lucas Lodge

A gathering to welcome the regiment to Meryton. Barouches at midnight. Not quite as fancy as St James's Court but we will have a capital time all the same! Join us for punch, witty chit-chat and perhaps a reel or two in the sitting room. We are delighted to be welcoming **Mr Darcy**, **Mr Bingley**, **Miss Caroline Bingley**, **Mr Hurst** and **Louisa Hurst** even though they don't go often to St James's Court – perhaps I could introduce them lol! Charlotte will be making her famous mince pies, so come hungry!

Mrs Bennet
Oh really, my daughters never do any cooking, what a shame for poor Charlotte, maybe that's why she is unwed?
#justsaying

Caroline Bingley
You are too kind, sir

Lydia Bennet
UMMM new officers hello

Sir William Lucas
And may I suggest **Lizzy Bennet** as a desirable dancing partner to **Fitzwilliam Darcy**

 Fitzwilliam Darcy
I would be very happy to dance with you, Miss Bennet

 Lizzy Bennet
Changed your tune! Think I'll sit this one out, thanks ;)

 Sir William Lucas
Fitzwilliam Darcy perhaps you've danced at St James's Court? I'm sure you must be fond of superior society. Do you have a house in town?

 Fitzwilliam Darcy
[Untag]

 Fitzwilliam Darcy
Is this working?

 Fitzwilliam Darcy
[Untag]

 Fitzwilliam Darcy
Why isn't this working?

29 October 1811

Caroline
This party succckkkkks

Oh God now they are singing 😶

Oh great, by all means let's dance a reel. In the sitting room

What a small room, hardly space for my head feathers

Charles talking to JB again. She's a sweetie but obviously . . . I mean . . . just no. THE MOTHER!! Can't we redirect him to someone more suitable?

Ugh let's just leave. Maybe I could mend your pen for you ;) ;)

Fitzwilliam
Pen? What? I mend my own, Caroline

Oh reeeeally

???

OMG just saw your tweet about fine eyes, may one dare ask whose eyes????

😂

OMG have an amazing time with your new mother-in-law!! She'll fit right in at Pemberley! Can't wait for the wedding! LOL

Oh you're serious? I am #allastonishment

29 October 1811

> **Fitzwilliam**
> Charles, why has your sister sent me a small miniature with the words 'this could be us but you playin' (on the pianoforte)'? I don't understand

> Also what should I do about Lizzy B? She looks nice tonight. I don't know why I said she wasn't hot, she actually is very tolerable indeed. Should I tell her I think so? Or laugh at one of her witticisms? Or just ignore her like they say to do online?

> Charles

> Charles!

> God, no point texting you while you're with Jane B, you look like that stupid heart-eyes etching you're always sending

 **Lizzy Bennet** Having a great night at Lucas Lodge but wondering what brings the regiment here, **Colonel Forster**, is Hertfordshire about to be invaded by the French?!

✓ *commended by **Fitzwilliam Darcy***

 Captain Carter
I hate the French 😠

 Lieutenant Denny
🏴󠁧󠁢󠁥󠁮󠁧󠁿 🏴󠁧󠁢󠁥󠁮󠁧󠁿 🏴󠁧󠁢󠁥󠁮󠁧󠁿

 Colonel Forster
LOL no we just need some down-time. Putting the mental in regimental, that's us

 Captain Carter
redcoatsredcoatsredcoats

29 October

Lizzy
OMG why is Mr D commending my comments? Weird. I mean he said I was barely tolerable and he never talks to me. So why now 'commend' stuff I say? What's his game? Also he does look good tonight. His breeches are SO TIGHT. Oh God forget I said that.

Charlotte?

Helloooo?

Charlotte
Can't talk up to elbows in mince pies

11 November 1811

Caroline
Jane babes! Louisa and I going totally insane in this tiny pokey mansion!!! Only three billiard rooms, I mean, I ask you. Come and have kitchen sups later. I'll get Nicholls to rustle up a quick five-course meal

Jane
Love to!! Thanks!! So nice of you!!

Charles isn't going to be here. Just FYI

Oh. That's totally fine. No probs. Was not even thinking he might be. Ha ha

Am sure I don't need to say this but remember to wear a proper head-dress, we actually dress for dinner here! Love ya babes kiss kiss

11 November 1811

Posted by **Mrs Bennet**
Need some advice ladies. ID (impoverished daughter) 1 has been invited to dine with the sisters of BAE (bachelor approaching engagement) but BAE will not be there, any ideas how to make the most of this?

Comment /**Mumofthree** If it looks like rain you could send her on foot or pony, then she might catch a cold and have to stay over

> **Reply by** /**Mrs Bennet** Great idea!

>> **Reply by** /**Lady Lucas** I don't know tbh, that sounds dangerous, a friend of a friend's daughter died of a cold she caught while walking to a luncheon party

>>> **Reply by** /**Mrs Bennet** Oh ur so sweet to worry about my Jane. I think I'll risk it though, after all people don't die of little trifling colds lol! Any suitors for your lot yet? Just wondering . . .

11 November 1811

Mrs Bennet
Oh what a shame it looks like 🌧, Jane will have to stay the night at Netherfield 😊

Lizzy
Seriously mum, she will get soaked, send the carriage!

Mrs Bennet
Your father needs the carriage on the farm, right my love??

Mr Bennet
Whatever you say dear 🙄

Jane
I am here guys

11 November 1811

Nicholls
OMG **@Hill** major goss. Your Miss Jane Bennet is 'sick' and installed in our fourteenth spare bedroom for the foreseeable! Did her mother try the old 'send her out in a rain shower' trick?

Hill
Lips are sealed m8

Nicholls
She's a sweet girl though of course no £££, but who'll have to bring up all the trays of broth, that's right muggins here

11 November 1811

16 ladies of your acquaintance do declare that they are hale and hearty following the recent light rain shower

Jane Bennet is feeling sniffly at **Netherfield Park**

Caroline Bingley Be assured we will nurse you back from this clearly debilitating mild cold

Mrs Bennet Poor Jane! Who could have foreseen this! Lucky she has the sweetest disposition ever, would make an excellent wife #justsaying

Charles Bingley Thoughts and prayers with all those caught in the latest light shower! #sodamp

Mary Bennet So sad that my dear sister Jane is so terribly wet for you sir. Still these things are sent to try us. Might I suggest a reading from Fordyce's Sermons?

Charles Bingley 😄

Charles Bingley Oh wait you're serious

12 November 1811

Charles
If you like drinking hot broth, and getting caught in the rain, I'm the gentleman with five thousand a year that you've looked for

Sorry, too soon?

Are you sure you don't have the plague? Is your cough dry or phlegmy?

Sorry TMI lol

Suck a lemon! I'll order one from London, it will only take three months if I pay for express delivery on **instafootman.com**

Got you a personalised bed jacket at **www.notonthemerytonhighstreet.com**

Also got some broths from Deliveroux

Are you OK? Shame I can't come in and see you. It would be most improper lol

. . . wouldn't it?

Point (A) *Longbourn*

⋮

Point (B) *Netherfield*

Walking distance from Longbourn to Netherfield: barely three miles

WARNING: *journey may involve stiles, rough terrain and six inches of mud!*

Lizzy Bennet @Lizzybennet

12 NOVEMBER 1811

#messyhairdontcare #petticoatsdeepnotlosingsleep
#brighteyesnolies

When you decide to walk instead of taking the
carriage . . . Looking forward to seeing **@janebennet**
and **@abingleybingbong** (and no one else LOL jk). I
love six inches . . . six inches of mud that is!
#alwaysinstile

The Etiquette Site for the Newly Elevated

UPDATE from carolineinthecountrysadly 12 November 1811

Thanks everyone for your thoughts on my original post, 'How to Get Rid of Unwanted Houseguests' – unfortunately your advice sucked, not only did that not work but now her sister is here too! And she is so pert too. Insolent really. Ugh! What can I do?

Comment /nobleandproud Just tell her someone's got plague

> **Reply by** /carolineinthecountrysadly The sick sister already thinks everyone has the plague, we've got a bulk order of lemons on the way ffs

Comment /accomplishedwoman83 Try only serving three varieties of game at dinner?

> **Reply by** /carolineinthecountrysadly Won't work. She's definitely used to that #lowconnections

Comment /mrsthorpe I had this friend once who stayed in a house with all these locked rooms and thought someone had been murdered there, that definitely got her out

> **Reply by** /carolineinthecountrysadly Serious answers only please. No one would be that dumb would they?

AskJane

Logged in: Caroline Bingley

SEARCH HISTORY

Can you get sick from a light rain shower

Q   How soon is it acceptable to get rid of a supposedly sick person from your house

How to tell if a man is falling in love with someone else

12 November 1811

Caroline
Can't believe Lizzy Bennet walked all the way here! The state of her hair!

Louisa
OMG her petticoats! Six inches deep in mud I swear

Caroline
I'm sure you wouldn't wish your sister to make such an exhibition **@Fitzwilliam**?

Fitzwilliam
No indeed

Caroline
Perhaps this will affect your enjoyment of her fine ••

Fitzwilliam
On the contrary, her eyes were brightened by the exercise

Caroline
Huh. Invited her to play Cards Against Society with us earlier and she turned us down for a book. A BOOK!

Louisa
Not convinced she knows how to play tbh. Bennet girls have zero accomplishments (unless you count extensive reading and muddy walks, LOL)

Caroline
I mean, how many ladies really are accomplished these days? (present chat excluded) 😘😘

Fitzwilliam
Can hardly think of any tbh

Charles
Rubbish! You're all constantly accomplishing things. You're brave to even get out of bed with all the colds and corsets you have to deal with (#ally). Anyway look at this new landau in *Your Barouche Box* magazine – is five really enough? Might be time to upgrade to the Landau Turbo 500? With alloy foot-men and in-built satnav (it's a new thing, comes with a coachman sat on top to navigate)

Mr Hurst
Will there be any sport?

In Stile

The Site for Excellent Walkers

Which walker are you . . .
a muddy scamper or a turn about the room?

Make the most of a walk
get that proposal

Cool off!
top ten bodies of water for jumping in

100 best mud-resistant petticoats

AskJane

Logged in: Fitzwilliam Darcy

SEARCH HISTORY

Q Ladies in muddy petticoats

Bright eyes

Hair really quite wild

13 November 1811

> **Fitzwilliam**
> Good day, Miss Bennet

> I trust your family are well.

> Do you often walk about the countryside with your hair so wild and your eyes so bright?

> BTW I meant to say sorry for that time at the ball when I wouldn't dance with you.

> Urgh

MESSAGES NOT DELIVERED

13 November 1811

Lizzy
URGH CHARLOTTE this place is the worst. Smug sisters want me at bottom of pond. Mr D super-weird and keeps staring at me, assume my dress is not 'fashion' enough for him or something. I read a book once for like ten mins (just to get away from Mr Hurst and his port-breath) and now they think I'm a bluestocking or something

Charlotte
Oh Mr D is staring at you is he?
Hmmmm

Oh stop it, we hate each other

Caroline Bingley
@carolineinthecity
Bio: London and Hertfordshire based. Sister, friend, socialite. Six foot in my head feathers.

Caroline Bingley @carolineinthecity
13 November 1811

Help us settle an argument please! Nowadays women are always claiming to be accomplished – every profile on **marrymyimpoverisheddaughter.com** for a start – but how many really are, and what does it truly mean to be accomplished? POLL!

☐ thorough knowledge of French
☐ a certain something in her manner and means of address
☐ playing and singing
☐ embroidering screens

 @englandtillldie Thorough knowledge of French?! Reporting this account for treason

 @abingleybingbong All of them! Everything! Ladies rock! #dontknowhowshedoesit

 @NapoleonBonerPart A certain something in her petticoats amirite?

@tradesmansdaughter Seriously check your #aristoprivilege not everyone has a screen to embroider

@puttingonthefitz Can think of maybe half a dozen at best. And I'd add improving her mind with extensive reading to your list

✓ Commended by **@carolineinthecity**

@pertopinionsfineeyes Wow no wonder you hardly know any accomplished women. We can't all be perfect!

> **@carolineinthecity** Perhaps you have not moved in society much? Lots of accomplished ladies that we know! #womensupportwomen #thisgirlcan(embroiderscreens)

> **@puttingonthefitz** Everyone has flaws, sure

> **@pertopinionsfineeyes** Like not dancing at balls? Being unimpressed with literally everything? Looking like you're always smelling something bad?

> **@puttingonthefitz** How about judging everyone the second you meet them?

> **@sirwilliamlucas** Jeez get a room you two!! ;) then take a turn about it LOL

> **@carolineinthecity** Just sitting down at the harpsichord if anyone fancies a livestream??

13 November 1811

@carolineinthecity
We have to get this woman out of the house. Darcy literally will not stop staring at her and now she's flirtatiously talking to him about philosophy or something, sooooo boring. I mean, who cares what the difference between pride and vanity is, so long as you have a decent floor-length mirror?

@easylouisa
Hang on, I'll go and play that really fast bit on the piano, that will shut her up

@carolineinthecity
DO IT, I'm gonna get her to take selfies with me but only use filters on myself

@easylouisa
Babe, you are such a pro

@carolineinthecity
So over these Bennets, really need to get Charles to marry Georgiana Darcy ASAP

Caroline Bingley @carolinebingley

14 NOVEMBER 1811

Good day friends! Delighted to support the campaign #booksaremyreticule – I have ten tote reticules to give away to keen readers such as myself! Made from the finest cotton, guaranteed free of serf labour (peasant-crafted). I do declare there is nothing like a book!

14 November 1811

@puttingonthefitz
Look, I don't think you got what I meant by accomplished

@puttingonthefitz
Sorry to 'ease into your private etchings' as I think they say

@puttingonthefitz
I have high standards but for myself as well, you know

@puttingonthefitz
Have you read The Seven Habits of Highly Effective Landowners? I'll send you a link

@puttingonthefitz
Hello?

@puttingonthefitz
Anyway, there is a difference between pride and vanity, you know. Here's a link to the wikialmanac explaining **www.wikialmanac. com/whatisvanity**

18 November 1811

Mr Bennet
I hope, my dear, you have ordered a good dinner today, for I have reason to expect a guest

Mrs Bennet
OMG Mr Bingley! And we've nothing decent in. Can we get some on instafootman?

Mr Bennet
It is not Mr Bingley, but someone who when I am dead may turn you all out of the house

Mrs Bennet
NOT PUFF-GUTS COLLINS??

Mr Bennet
Please give poor Cousin William the respect he deserves. Which, judging by this letter, is not a great deal. But still.

Lydia
PUFF-GUTS 💀

Mrs Bennet
Coming to measure up for curtains
is he? And not a daughter married
yet. I even tried the 'rain shower'
trick and still NOTHING, no one
cares about my poor nerves

Mr Bennet
He sent me his V-Harmony profile,
before you completely write him
off. You know, the site for vicars
who want to marry in the next two
to three weeks . . .

Mrs Bennet
OMG HE'S IN THE MARKET???

Mrs Bennet
THIS. IS. HUGE.

Mrs Bennet
NO ONE INTRODUCE HIM TO
CHARLOTTE LUCAS

Mr Bennet
He's also sent me a link to some
very detailed travel plans and a link
to his website
www.thisvicaragelife.com

Lizzy
This can't be real surely? I am
deceased. I have died.

Jane
Come on guys, he's probably really
sweet and it's not his fault we live
in sexist times

Lizzy
You are way too good Jane. It's not
you who'll have to marry him is it,
since you're already halfway up the
aisle according to Mum

Jane
OMG STOP shhhhh 💀

AskJane

SEARCH HISTORY

Is it legal to marry your daughter off to her cousin who will inherit an entailed house

How to subtly steer conversation towards men marrying your daughters

What do vicars eat

18 November 1811

Posted by **Mrs Bennet**
More help needed ladies, the inheritor of my EE (entailed estate) is coming to stay, think he will wed one of my ID (impoverished daughters) but which one? ID1 may be very soon engaged. ID2 wilful and obstinate. IDs4 and 5 total slappers. ID3 plain but could be prevailed upon?? Any advice please, fellow mums?

Comment /**Lady Lucas** Following with interest ●●

This Vicarage Life

*I'm not a regular vicar,
I'm a fun vicar!*

by **Mr Collins** sponsored by **Lady Catherine de Bourgh**

About me
My noble patroness, Lady Catherine de Bourgh
Marriage aims (set example, secure happiness and
most importantly please my patroness!)
'Comping' – the art of paying little compliments to ladies!
Gardening with reverence
Chimney pieces of the world
Virtual tour of Rosings Park
On the Right Cath – My Lady Catherine de Bourgh fansite
Buy my ebook – The Happy Knack of Adapting to Society!
Subscribe to my podcast! This Vicarage Life
Support me on Patreoness! And thanks to my biggest donor,
Lady Catherine de Bourgh

THIS VICARAGE LIFE PODCAST
Episode List

Entail-igence: Everything you need to know about being the recipient of an entail! Featuring hot topics such as: should you bring it up in front of the entailees when a house guest? Is it a good reason to marry your cousin? And how soon is too soon to move in your furniture? PLUS an interview with my noble patroness, Lady Catherine de Bourgh!

Social sin-tercourse?: All your questions about social gatherings answered! Is it proper for clergymen to attend balls? Is dancing a sin? And should you ever approach fellow guests without an introduction? PLUS an interview with my noble patroness, Lady Catherine de Bourgh!

Decent Proposal: My top-ten tips! Including, how to know when no does not mean no, and the best techniques for discreet affection transference between ladies. PLUS an interview with my noble patroness, Lady Catherine de Bourgh!

Let us play!: Making the most of your leisure time, including: walking for fitness – how not to overdo it. Music – an innocent diversion? Whist – is it acceptable? PLUS an interview with my noble patroness, Lady Catherine de Bourgh!

Sin-terior décor: The dos and don'ts of furnishing. Shelves in the closet, yes or no? How to avoid chimney-shaming, and when to compare things to rooms at Rosings Park (hint – always). PLUS an interview with my noble patroness, Lady Catherine de Bourgh!

18 November 1811

Lydia
PSA hot new beau in town:
**www.plentyofredcoats.com/
georgewickhamesq**

Kitty
UMMMMM hello

Joining the reg next week fyi

yessss love a man in regimentals!

← → www.plentyofredcoats.com/georgewickhamesq + ⯗

George Wickham, 27
Cheerful young man, thriving despite great
misfortunes. Doing my best to live in harmony
with nature and the planet #namaste. Cannot
bear to be idle. Into meditation, hikes, spirituality and respecting women. Don't mind a night
of supper and cards once in a while LOL but
never miss breeches day at the gym!

Click here for my gopatroniseme page

– rewards include private spirituality coaching, a personalised painting
of your aura, and a video of me reading your favourite poem in a
sultry voice

William Collins has checked in at **Longbourn** ✈
Thanks for having me **Mrs Bennet**, thrilled to meet
your five amiable daughters and probably marry
one of them, only ethical thing to do IMHO

Mrs Bennet Thanks!! You're very very welcome!!! FYI Jane is
taken

*Reproached by **Fitzwilliam Darcy***

Lizzy Bennet FFS Mum

William Collins is delighted to discover that
Fitzwilliam Darcy is the nephew of his noble
patroness **Lady Catherine de Bourgh**!

Fitzwilliam Darcy I'm sorry, who are you?

Lizzy Bennet Oh God. Sorry, Mr Darcy, Mr Collins
is our cousin, he's new around here

Fitzwilliam Darcy Oh right. Makes sense he's
your cousin

Lizzy Bennet Um what's that supposed to mean?

Fitzwilliam Darcy Nothing

 **Lydia Bennet** and **Kitty Bennet** are now friends with **George Wickham**

 **Lydia Bennet** When's the next ball? It's been soooooo long. **CharlesBingley** tag you're it!

 Charles Bingley Bring it onnnn! All back to mine for white soup and tuuuuunes

 Mary Bennet UGH balls

 **Lizzy Bennet** is now friends with **George Wickham**

*Reproached by **Fitzwilliam Darcy***

 Upcoming event: **Supper and Cards** hosted by **Mrs Philips**

19 November 1811

Lizzy
Char have you met the new guy yet? He's sooo nice

Charlotte
Wickham? No not yet

We bumped into him in town just now. Ugh saw Darcy as well. Seemed to be weird vibes there, like they know each other, but not in a good way . . .

19 November 1811

> **Fitzwilliam**
> Dear Miss Elizabeth Bennet, saw
> you chatting to George Wickham
> in the street and just wanted to say

> Dear Miss Bennet, remember how
> we were talking the other day
> about my resentful temper, etc.
> Well

MESSAGES NOT DELIVERED

NOV
Supper and Cards
20
1811

Host - Mr and Mrs Philips
6pm–10pm
Chez Philips

Join us for supper and cards! Nothing special, just supper and cards. Bring who you like! It's only supper and cards. We shall have a laugh.

Remember, what is divulged to you at supper and cards stays at supper and cards.

Have fun! It's just supper and cards.

#suppercardslaughs

Lydia Bennet
Here you go **George Wickham** – come for some supper and cards

George Wickham
Like etchings and chill lol?

Lydia Bennet
ROFLLLLLLL no actually just supper and cards.
Come, it'll be fun! I'll take you on at lottery tickets ;)

Mrs Philips

ur all very welcome xxx LOL (lots of love) YOUR AUNT

William Collins

Would love to come! Thanks for having us to tea yesterday btw, really enjoyed your chimney piece. Like a 1/500 miniature model of one at Rosings 🔥 owned by my noble patroness **Lady Catherine de Bourgh** Is it a copy? The cards are fine with me btw even though I'm a clergyman. A recent episode of my podcast deals with exactly this sort of thing.

20 November 1811

George
Heyyyy Lizzy, guess who? 😃

You gonna be at supper and cards tonight?

Lizzy
Sure! Height of the social scene around here

Would be really nice to chat more. You probably wondered why me and Darcy were shooting daggers at each other before.

Oh, I dunno, didn't really notice

Can I send you something?

www.noimdefinitelynottheaddle-pate.com/keptfromthepulpit

NIDNTA (No I'm Definitely Not The Addlepate)
The Forum for the Cruelly Used

1 April 1811

Posted by **@keptfromthepulpit**

OK deep breath. Have told this to a few people and been advised to go more public, but keeping this anon for now.

This is about a guy I'll call Stick Up The Breeches (SUTB, 27M) and his sister PAD/Proud And Disagreeable (16F).

So me (27M) and SUTB used to be childhood mates, did all the usual stuff like poking sticks in rivers and wearing matching doublets, even though his dad was a total aristo and mine worked for him (#humble).

His dad really loved me and promised I could have a job in the church one day, which I was TOTALLY INTO (#spiritual #selflove #affirmation #goodvibes). Tragically, after he died (I was absolutely devastated, SUTB and PAD did not care AT ALL) SUTB totally refused to let me have the job, even though it was in his father's will!!! I was left completely destitute, both in terms of cash and my faith in the human condition tbh.

Tried to rise above it all and have joined the army now, fighting for my country like a legend (#mindfulness #positivity #healing) and I absolutely believe in #karma (#namaste) so I know it'll come back on them. In the meantime I'm just struggling to forgive and forget, y'know? Which is totally not good for my vibes. Any thoughts on what to do? Or if you want to chip into my **www.gopatroniseme.com**, I could really do with some funds to help rebuild my life!

20 November 1811

> **Lizzy**
> WOW

George
Yeah I know, it's a lot. Hope it's not a bit TMI.

> Not at all, I'm just so shocked by it all. Although not really. Hate that Darcy guy. He thinks he's so great just because he is super-rich and I guess 'handsome' in like a really obvious way.

LOL

> God we should tell people

Would you mind not? Remember 'what happens at supper and cards' etc LOL. I don't want to put out any bad vibes y'know?

> 💜 You're going to this ball Mr Bingley has planned right?

Wouldn't miss it. He's invited all the lads which tbf is really decent of him

See you there. I'll be the one in the redcoat 😛

AskJane

Logged in: Lizzy Bennet

SEARCH HISTORY

Average income soldier militia corps 1811

Q How much do you really need to live on
and be happy

Legal recourse if denied promised vicar
inheritance

Bonnet-A-Porter @bonnetaporter

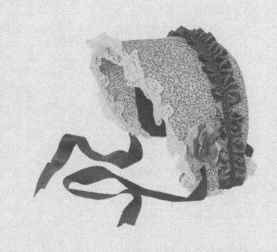

21 NOVEMBER 1811

SPONSORED AD
Sale now on!
Use the code 'latestfashions' for a guinea off longer
sleeves! #elegantandobliging

20 November 1811

Nicholls
Are you kidding me? Apparently we're hosting a ball now

Hill
When??

Nicholls
Depends when we've made enough white soup, Bingers says. And you can guess who gets that job, that's right, muggins here.

Sarah
Have you ever tried doing hair and make-up for five unmarried women?

20 November 1811

Posted by /Tradesmansdaughter67
Seeking marriage, no time-wasters! One hundred pounds a year and possibility of inheriting my father's carting business on his demise. If you don't hate the French, SWIPE LEFT!

Comment /NapoleonBonerPart Hey baby. Send me a nude self-etching please

> Reply by /Tradesmandaughter67 Who are you? This is a serious website for tradesmen's daughters and those who want to wed them. I'm reporting this account

>> Reply by /NapoleonBonerPart I've got something else you can report baby

From: info@damntediouswasteofaneveningevents.com
To: MrBennet@regularcorrespondence.com
Subject: You're going to Netherfield tonight!
Sent: 26 November 1811

Dear Mr Bennet,

Your Family Ticket (two wed, five unwed) for the Netherfield Ball is attached – please self-etch this QR code at home and present it to your host.

Please observe the following etiquette:

- Socially distance from anyone you have not been formally introduced to.
- One white soup only per attendee.
- Young ladies may exhibit one piece each upon the pianoforte.
- Conversation to be confined to recent social intercourse, furnishings and appointments, the dance including music, formation and number of couples. NB if you can't think of anything appropriate to say you will please restrict your remarks to the weather. All speculative wedding talk to be kept at a low volume so as not to cause embarrassment.
- Ms Caroline Bingley has requested that female guests be informed that the height of her head feathers shall be three-quarters of a yard; no ladies to match or exceed this height please. All chandeliers have been raised accordingly.

Have fun!

Lizzy Bennet
@pertopinionsfineeyes
Bio: Second of five daughters.
Likes walking, winking and
witticisms. She/Her

Lizzy Bennet @pertopinionsfineeyes
26 November 1811

Me: *makes an effort for once*
Mum: You'll never be as pretty as your sister
Jane but you do actually look quite nice!
Me: 😕
✓ *commended by* ***@abingleybingbong***

Lizzy Bennet @pertopinionsfineeyes
26 November 1811

Sister 4: You look nice
Me: Thanks
Sister 4: You better not dance with
[REDACTED] all night ok beatch?
Me: 💀

 @carolineinthecity Don't worry hun, vintage is
in this season, aww I had a dress like yours five
years ago only it was silk not cotton. You're so
#brave wearing it! #preloved #byalotofpeople

26 November 1811

Lizzy
Hey, are you here? Saw a redcoat but tbh there are dozens. Why do you guys all dress alike?

LOL

Looking forward to that dance you promised me, have stocked up on my store of amiable conversation!

Hello??

26 November 1811

Caroline
Just a heads-up babe, I hear you're quite delighted with George Wickham but maybe you don't know his dad was like a steward or something gross? Speaks for itself really doesn't it? All sorts of gossip about him back in Derbyshire . . .

Lizzy
Sigh. Don't believe everything you read on social intercourse sites ok?

26 November 1811

Charlotte
Soooo. Mr D looking hot tonight.
Has been staring at you since you
came in FYI.

Lizzy
Please. So not interested. Have you
seen Wickham?

This again? Liz, he hasn't got a bean
and neither have you, not exactly a
solid plan is it? Also he hasn't even
bothered to show up, whereas Mr D
is here and staring at you.

Stop it, Wickham's nice! Also I
don't want to stab him in the eye
with a fork whenever I see him.
Major plus.

Hun you need to be sensible about
this.

Right so I'm supposed to just find a
complete a-hole with cash and
suppress the urge to pick up a fork
every time he walks into the room.

What about Mr Collins? He seems pretty into you! Would definitely sort out the whole future housing issue . . .

Gonna assume that was a joke

Why not?!

Um, have you met him? UGH think you might be right about him being into me though, literally can't get rid of him. Already had to dance the first two with him.

Heads up, intense Darcy staring action at 5 o'clock.

God what is his deal? UGH hate that guy so much. Especially after what he did to Wickham

Yeah yeah but 10k a year goes a long way to excuse a bit of vicarage-blocking. And why are you taking Wickham's word for it all? You're not THAT into him are you? You're not actually thinking about . . .?? 💍

No! Maybe. UGGH.

Come on, this isn't like you to have so little sense! Speaking of which, what's Jane doing with Mr Bingley? Should be showing more affection than she feels, not less! You've gotta admit she's a bit 'resting indifference face' you know?

GAH gotta run, Darcy's coming over

INTERESTING

Charlotte!! Quick, come over and talk about poor people or something so he leaves. Char! You better not leave me with him so help me

The Daily Gossip

26 November 1811

Sidebar of scandal
Reporter J. Austen at this evening's exclusive Netherfield Ball

VERY FORWARD AT FIFTEEN
Miss Lydia Bennet flaunts her embonpoint in a daring ankle-length muslin **CLICK HERE FOR MORE**

WANT OF PROPRIETY
Visiting clergyman brazenly talks to noted aristocrat, compares all to Rosings Park **CLICK HERE FOR MORE**

WE WISH YOU WOULD SLUMBER, DEAR MAID
Unwelcome singing from least attractive Bennet sister **CLICK HERE FOR MORE**

CONSPICUOUS BY ABSENCE
Which redcoat failed to turn up to the social event of the season? **CLICK HERE TO FIND OUT THE SCANDALOUS REASON WHY!**

LOVE IS IN THE STUFFY AIR

Has Jane Bennet (one thousand in the 4 per cents only) sealed the deal with Bingley (£5k a year)? 'What congratulations will then flow in!' says local dignitary Sir William Lucas **CLICK HERE FOR MORE**

SHE SWORE SHE'D NEVER DANCE WITH HIM

Debatable local beauty Eliza Bennet, EE (estate entailed), stands up with Derbyshire heartthrob and the bachelor everyone loves to hate Fitzwilliam Darcy (£10k a year); they talk by rule **CLICK HERE FOR MORE**

MRS GORDON BENNET

Local mother of five embarrasses room with awkward marriage chat **CLICK HERE FOR MORE**

Lizzy Bennet
@pertopinionsfineeyes
Bio: Second of five daughters.
Likes walking, winking and
witticisms. She/Her

Lizzy Bennet @pertopinionsfineeyes
26 November 1811

How to talk while dancing
Me: What a lot of couples eh
Dance BAE: Yeah

(brief awkward pause of seven thousand
hours)

Dance BAE: At least the room is big
Me: Yeah
✓ *commended by @puttingonthefitz*

26 November 1811

George
U up?

Sorry didn't make it to ball after all.
Didn't want to see Darcy tbh –
thought some absolute #scenes
might arise

Lizzy
Oh no worries. Was a fun night. Had
to dance with Darcy though, LOL

Oh right. You didn't mention that
forum post I sent you, did you?

Well I kind of hinted I knew he did
you out of your vicarship even
though his dad wanted you to have
it. Nothing major. Someone should
call him out though! Absolutely
twattish behaviour

Look, I really got on with his dad, I
just can't bring myself to expose
his son like that. I'm moving on with
my life. #positivevibesonly

Wow. Don't think I could be so chill about it. I just think everyone needs to know what an absolute arse he is. Does it not make you mad? I mean, you might want the money if you ever need it for . . . any particular reason

God I don't know, like maybe you want to get married or any other random example

Yeah yeah. But karma will sort all that.

Not sure karma is as effective as a short sharp Witterstorm but fine, your call

The Support Group for Landowners Drawn to Young Ladies with Low Connections

Posted by **derbyshirelad** 27 November 1811

Advice needed, chaps. I (27M) find myself kind of into a young lady (20F) of reduced means and inferior connections (her cousin talked to me when he hadn't been introduced – pretty serious stuff like that). I mean, can you imagine? But damn, her eyes are so fine. And her opinions so pert. What should I do? Marriage not really an option as her mother/sisters/dad are way too common and anyway I'm supposed to marry my cousin (27F) (long story). I should put her down as much as possible and get away from the neighbourhood, right?

Comment /Ilikebigparksandlcannotlie Bro chew your leg out of the bear trap asap, no way do you want to be inviting your uncultured mother-in-law round every Yuletide talking over the Regent's speech and stuff

William Collins Can't wait to marry **Lizzy Bennet**! Invites will be sent shortly, wedding will include a private tour of Rosings Park!! #bounty-andbeneficence

Charlotte Lucas
Oh wow! Congratulations!!

Mrs Bennet
So thrilled! Oh don't worry **Charlotte Lucas** I'm sure it won't be too long now for you!

Lizzy Bennet
HA HA what a great prank Cousin William. You forget I have not given you my answer. Have sent you a PM – please read and don't post anything else OK?

William Collins

William Collins got engaged to **Lizzy Bennet**. Thanks to **Mrs Bennet** AKA the mother-in-law2be for the not-so-subtle hints LOL

Lizzy Bennet What? No no you didn't! I said no! I literally just said it

William Collins Assumed that was a joke, haha. It's not like you're likely to get another offer, so . . .

Lizzy Bennet OK, tempting though this whole thing is, just to reiterate, NO.

William Collins So elegant 💜 Call me when you can, we need to talk about table decorations.

John Glassblower We all know that no means yes when it comes to ladies and proposals, amirite?

William Collins Indeed! It's tip 4/10 on a recent episode of This Vicarage Life – perhaps you are a listener sir?

Mrs Bennet Hahahaa you're welcome dear sir, don't listen to Lizzy, she is so obstinate. Of course she wants to be your wife

Lizzy Bennet NO, NO I DON'T.

William Collins Oh dear, obstinacy is no. 3 in Lady Catherine's list of unsuitable traits for a wife. Um maybe this was a bad idea

Mrs Bennet No I mean obstinate in a cute way. Please marry her.

 Mrs Bennet Lizzy I SWEAR TO GOD I WILL NEVER SPEAK TO YOU AGAIN IF YOU MESS THIS UP

 Mr Bennet Well well. An unhappy choice between your parents is ahead of you Lizzy . . .

 Mrs Bennet FFS MR BENNET U HAVE NO COMPASSION FOR MY NERVES

Charlotte Lucas @charlottelucas

30 NOVEMBER 1811

Wedding bells! I'm really happy to announce my engagement to the Reverend William Collins **@thefunvicar** #comfortablehome #alllask #notromanticneverwas

@lizzybennet OMG! That's amazing, congrats you guys . . . I guess it's all worked out for the best 💀

@thefunvicar #happiestofmen!! Wait till you see the chimney piece at Rosings! It's worth marrying me for that alone LOL

@mrsbennet Are you effing kidding me Charlotte?

30 November 1811

> **Lizzy**
> Charlotte what the HELL?!

Charlotte
What? You were done with him right? You sounded really happy for us on my post!

> Are you seriously doing this?

Oh right, you didn't want him so why would anyone? Look, I'm not a hearts-and-flowers type you know, like Jane – just wanted somewhere to live that's not with my mum making mince pies till I die

> Hun, I know. It's just . . . what are you going to talk about??

Oh, I dunno, Rosings Park? Chimney pieces?

> Jeez mate

Honestly, this is what I want. Can't you just be happy for me?

Lizzy?

> Of course I can. Honestly *hugs*

30 November 1811

Lady Lucas
Hi babes do you have the floor plans for Longbourn?

Mrs Bennet
Seriously?? No one around here has any compassion for my nerves. Bloody Lizzy, so obstinate.

Oh I know it will be AGES before Charlotte and dear William can move in. Just being organised!

How's Mr B by the way? Hope still well and strong? Looked a bit peaky the other day, that's all

You're so sweet to ask! He's never been better actually. Probably live forever at this rate! Thriving. It's all the long walks he takes in our extensive gardens. And all the stairs. In the house. Which is our house.

Anyway, you must be thrilled Charlotte is finally married off at her advanced age. We all thought she'd be stuck making pastries for your small social gatherings forever.

Yes, well, she didn't want to rush into anything too soon. Being so demure, you know. Actually I suppose with your lot you don't know.

Anyway, it's all fine because Jane is going to land Mr Bingley any day now

Oh no, you didn't hear?

Oh God, what?

Apparently they're off to town. No plans to return. Soz

Charles Bingley @abingleybingbong

30 NOVEMBER 1811

📌 **Nice Part of London, not Cheapside**

Lol on the move again! Love the country but also the city!
Happy wherever I am! #worldtraveller #nondigitalnomad
#SPON Always use my fave Portmanteau Inc luggage!
For the discerning gentlemen of no fixed estate!

Jane Bennet 🙁

Mrs Bennet Dearest Mr Bingley, you've not left? ur
coming back soon though right?

Mrs Bennet Right?

Caroline Bingley @carolinebingley

30 NOVEMBER 1811

So happy to be back in London – won't miss much about Hertfordshire! Can't even get langoustines! Can't wait to see **@georgianadarcy** my BFF (bosom friend forever) and practically sister! (Not quite sister yet but am I wrong to entertain hopes **@abingleybingbong**? 😒)

 **Jane Bennet** is now listening to **Miss Lizzo** on **StringQuartetify**

 Jane Bennet Why gentlemen great till they gotta be great??

 Jane Bennet Don't mean to be so negative SORRY

 Jane Bennet If you love someone, set them free (to go to London)

25 December 1811

 **Jane Bennet** is now reading **Ladies Who Esteem Too Greatly**. 178 pages read on **Commendablereads**

The Forum for Slighted Young Ladies

Posted by **janeb** 29 December 1811

Ladies, hoping for a bit of comfort. The man everyone said was in love with me and about to propose has gone to London and looks like he won't come back. I don't understand what I did – was I in an unflattering gown, or did I mention entails too many times? Thought he'd at least send a Christmas card, but nothing!

Comment /slightedinswindon Hmmm babe, if you weren't engaged then I dunno what you can do. Nothing to reproach him with innit

Comment /unluckyinlove Did you get your mum to go on mumsofunweddaughters for tips? Did you show more affection than you felt? Did you get caught in a rain shower deliberately then stay at his house for weeks?

> **Reply by /slightedinswindon** Yeah the men know about that one now

Comment /honeyplease Has he pulled the old 'business in London' nonsense? Babe, don't follow him to London whatever you do, it's a bit desperate. Work on yourself first. Have you read Dine, Reflect, Connect?

30 December 1811

Jane Bennet has checked in at **Gracechurch Street, London** ✈

3 January 1812

> **Lizzy**
> All settled in London then?

Jane
Lizzy! So nice to hear from you. Yes thanks, Aunt and Uncle Gardiner are so sweet and the kids are adorbs

> Any sign of . . .?

Sent Caroline a few texts but no reply

> Shocker

They're probably really busy

> Yeah yeah

I'm sure she'll tell Charles I'm here anyway and we'll see

> I wish I was so sure

5 January 1812

Charles
Thought I saw Miss Jane Bennet on Gracechurch St today as I was landauing past – anyone know if she's in town?

Louisa
No, pretty sure I saw her posting about being in Bonnets R Us in Meryton

Caroline
Look at this pic of Georgiana looking hot.

Can't wait to see her

Fitzwilliam
Eww, please Caroline, she's my sister and she's 16

9 January 1812

Jane
Hey babe, did you not get my texts
last week? I'm in London!!

Caroline
Oh, my phone wasn't working

Oh, well I'm here, at Gracechurch Street

Never heard of it. In what part of
London is Gracechurch Street?

Cheapside

Oh sure, I'll give you a shout babe,
really busy with dear Georgiana
right now xxx

Great, let's get coffee at
StarGuineas one day maybe

Hmm OK. Just think it's really
important to support our English
coffee right now babes xxx just did
a post on it last week

Thought your phone wasn't working

3 February 1812

Mrs Collins
Hey hey, sorry not been in touch, absolutely manic planning the wedding and move to Kent. All OK with you?

Lizzy
Yeah fine

Look, I know what you're thinking

Char, it's fine, I get it, you had to do what you had to do

Will you come and stay at the parsonage once I'm settled? I know you're not exactly a Mr C fan, but . . . Dad and Maria are coming soon, love to see you too

I miss you . . .

Yes of course

Only if I get a private tour of Rosings Park tho OK? ;)

Just you try to avoid it and see what happens

@happythoughtindeed

1 MARCH 1812

Happy Thought Indeed (the magazine for interior decoration ideas)

Make sure to get this month's issue for an exclusive peep at Hunsford Parsonage, recently redecorated by the Reverend and Mrs Collins. From shelves in the closet to a drawing room at the back of the house, this bijou parsonage bursts with innovative style and modern conveniences.

@sirwilliamlucas The staircase is eminently suitable! Coincidentally at St James's Court there is also a staircase

@thefunvicar Fun fact, this is modelled on one of the staircases at Rosings Park! I say staircases, for there are several

@jillrandom Not the only thing in the closet perhaps

@lordangryson Can't believe no one is talking about the window tax, typical of the mainstream media 'MSM'

@lizzybennet Looking forward to coming to stay!

 **Lizzy Bennet** has checked in at **Rosings Park, Kent** ✈
11 March 1812

Excited to finally see this place and its 105 windows, after all I've heard about it 😎

 Sir William Lucas Not bad eh? Really happy my Charlotte's done so well for herself. Talk about a #fortunatealliance!

 Sir William Lucas Umm didn't mean anything by that #awks

 Maria Lucas Eeeep cannot believe we are actually going I am so scared gonna 😣

 Mrs Gardiner Not as nice as Derbyshire!

 Mrs Philips Hope u are havin fun Lizzy LOL aunt philips xxx

 Mr Bennet Well well, off gallivanting again Lizzy? No thought for your poor old dad

 William Collins Hey cuz, probably you were just excited to visit but there are actually 107 windows OK?

 Fitzwilliam Darcy Oh, that's my aunt's house. Did you know?

 Fitzwilliam Darcy Good luck with her is all I can say 'L.O.L'

Fitzwilliam Darcy But seriously, why are you there?

 Lizzy Bennet Lucky for me I can travel where I like, unlike certain other people who have been reduced to poverty through no fault of their own!

 Fitzwilliam Darcy What?

18 March 1812

> **Fitzwilliam**
> Hello, Lizzy

> Good day, Miss Bennet

> Hope your family is well?

MESSAGES NOT DELIVERED

19 March 1812

> Saw a nice footpath today and thought of you

> You know, because of all the walking

MESSAGES NOT DELIVERED

21 March 1812

> Hello, are you still in Kent? I was thinking of coming to visit my aunt

MESSAGES NOT DELIVERED

24 March 1812

Lizzy
So here I am in Kent, trying to pretend I'm prostrate with joy at visiting Rosings Park and keep poor Char from killing her new hubs, and guess who shows up??

Jane
OMG not . . .

Bingo. Up Himself Darcy indeed. I mean seriously, is he following me around or something? No, that doesn't make sense, he hates me.

Probably he's just visiting his aunt

Urgh yeah. But then why does he keep showing up at the parsonage?

Maybe he's just trying to be nice!

It's weird. He keeps showing up to chat, then not saying anything. He's got his cousin with him who seems nice anyway. Will try to pump for info about Mr B xxx

Lady Catherine de Bourgh
@herladyship
Bio: One of the most cultured ladies in England, with the finest taste in music. Britain's most skilled pianist (should I have ever learned). Mother, aunt, landowner, hostess. I must have my share in the online conversation!

Lady Catherine de Bourgh
@herladyship
24 March 1812

It has come to my attention that in some families the younger daughters are out before the elder are married. Let that sink in. ALL FIVE OUT AT ONCE. Here's the problem with that. THREAD (1/650)

25 March 1812

Fitzwilliam
Good day

Family all well?

29 March 1812

Perambulated on this great road today. Don't you just love 50 miles of good road?

Guess that's about how far away we are from Longbourn where you live, haha. Pemberley much further away though

You know, just saying

You should come!

Pemberley, I mean. Loads of great walks, you'd definitely like it

Lots of chances to get your petti-coat muddy

I do apologise, madam.
Over-familiarity.

Trust your family are well?

Sorry for all the texts!

29 March 1812

Lizzy
Seriously, there's like 100 texts now, what is going on? I don't understand him. First he says I'm an uggo, then he asks me to dance, now he's sending all these messages and watching me play the piano and stuff, but also hardly talks to me URGH MEN

Jane
Sounds like he's being kind of nice?

Maybe on the surface yeah, but can't get past what he did to Wickham

Wickham who's gone off with an heiress?

Well yes OK but he has to live off something

Perhaps Darcy has caught a terrible fever after a short rain shower? OMG or the plague! You should suck a lemon quick if you went within one metre of him. I read it's being spread by the new high-speed telegram network

Jane hun, I know you're sad about Mr Bingley but you've got to stop reading these plague conspiracy sites

14 April 1812

Colonel Fitzwilliam
Hey there 😄

Just wanted to say sorry about Darcy being so weird this afternoon. Talk about awks!

Lizzy
It's fine, I'm used to it

Oh really? He was like this in Hertfordshire then? Always wondered what he's like when he's hanging out with strangers

Ummm

Wow that bad huh? He's not such a bad guy. Just . . . not exactly a conversationalist, LOL. Bet he refused to dance with anyone, haha.

No comment . . .

He's way easier to talk to if you just know him a bit better!

Guess that explains Bingley. Always wondered why they're such mates. Do you know Mr B? Hear he might be in London for a while huh?

Oh yeah they're really tight, him and Cousin Darcy. Haha, he even saved Bingley from that total relationship fail!

Oh really?

Yeah, I heard Bingley was practically about to propose to some girl who was hella unsuitable. Think Darcy convinced him to go to London, then managed to convince Bingley she just wasn't that into him and he should find someone else. #crueltobekind

Add me on snapbavardage OK! And check out my ThouTube channel for my latest business ideas – you can get 10 per cent off my online sunglasses shop The Shades of Pemberley

WTF? Go back to the bit about Bingley.

Oh, about the girl Bingley was going to marry but she had an awful family and no money so Darcy split them up?

Yeah that

- 125 -

16 April 1812

Fitzwilliam
Greetings, madam. Is this your
number?

Sorry, it's just you weren't replying

Look, I just really need to talk to you

I know it's foolish because you hate
me and you're absolutely pennil

Argh pressed send too early

Absolutely *lovely*

But you are penniless too, you have
to admit. And your family's kind of
a nightmare

Thing is, I don't actually care
though, because you are just so
lovely and I think maybe I might
highly esteem you or something?

Lizzy, please reply. I really think I
might love you. Ardently even

Please will you marry me? Like seriously. I love you

Lizzy
Leave me alone. Delete my number

What?

Lizzy?

Seriously, get in the sea

What? We are several miles inland

I think I have some distant cousins in the Admiralty but that's about it

Look, this was actually really hard for me

No need to be so harsh

I mean, God, do you know how many young ladies would lose their mind to have a major landowner propose to them over text?

Did you mess with Jane and Bingley?

Of what are you talking?

Did you tell Bingley Jane wasn't that into him and talk him into going to London and never seeing her again?

No

OK, yes, but it was for their own good. For both of them. She really didn't seem that into him and I didn't want to see him hurt. Plus all the penniless/mad relations things. I wish I'd done the same for myself tbh but here we are

U still there?

I know what you did to Wickham

Sorry?

www.nidnta.com/ keptfromthepulpit

What the devil is that?! AM I SUTB??

You're the last man I'd ever marry. Even if you weren't such an arrogant tosser in yourself, you've hurt my sister and I can't forgive you for that

Is this because I made my proposals over text? I'm sorry if I hurt your pride, OK. Can we talk?

TBH the mode of your declaration just made it easier to say no

Jesu Christ, bit mean

You have blocked Fitzwilliam Darcy.

16 April 1812

> **Lizzy**
> So you know how I said Mr Collins's proposal was the worst proposal ever . . .?

Jane
. . . yes because it was

> And it wasn't possible to imagine anyone being ruder and more insulting whilst also proposing?

No, that does not seem possible . . . LOL unless it was by text!!

> Funny story

OMG did Mr Darcy propose?!!

> How did you know?

Oh come on. All those messages. And he kept turning up and then being too shy to speak to you. It was totally obvious! Ohhhh poor Mr Darcy. Assuming you said no?

> I dare say he'll survive

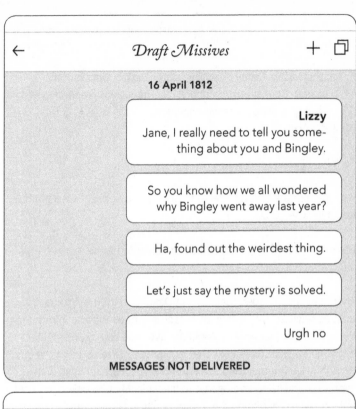

16 April 1812

Lizzy
Jane, I really need to tell you something about you and Bingley.

So you know how we all wondered why Bingley went away last year?

Ha, found out the weirdest thing.

Let's just say the mystery is solved.

Urgh no

MESSAGES NOT DELIVERED

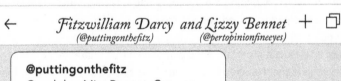

Fitzwilliam Darcy *and* *Lizzy Bennet*
(@puttingonthefitz) *(@pertopinionfineeyes)*

@puttingonthefitz
Good day, Miss Bennet. Can you follow me so I can 'direct message' you? Thanks.

OK fine, I'll email you. Is this you, **ElizabethBennet91@ regularcorrespondence.com**?

This message could not be sent as this user does not follow you

From: Fitzwilliam Darcy (fitzwilliamdarcyesq@quothnet.com)
To: Elizabeth Bennet (elizabethbennet91@regularcorrespondence.com)
Subject: My dealings with Mr Wickham
Sent: 17 April 1812

To Miss Elizabeth Bennet,

Be not alarmed! I'm not intending to propose again. (I save that for text missives, 'L.O.L' . . .)

Please pardon this lengthy email. I just wanted to set some things straight . . .

First of all, I've flagged that 'No I'm Definitely Not the Addlepate' post as misleading. Quite a lot of factually questionable information there. There is just no way Wickham ever had any intention of becoming a vicar (seriously, that is hilarious, have you met the guy?). When my dear father died, Mr Wickham requested a cash sum instead of the living and used it to invest in what he called 'a tasteful artistic project exploring the contours of the female form'. I only wish that had raised more red flags at the time. I attach a link to his anonymous profiles on various sites. Sorry you will have to view so many bare ankles, but I feel you should know his true character (yes, I'm afraid he is the 'NapoleonBonerPart' who has been posting throughout the internet. Ugh.)

This leads me to a rather touchy subject. Unfortunately, after convincing her that he was raising money for missionary work in Hull, Wickham managed to persuade my sister Georgiana into an etching session last year. She thought it was some kind of *Calendar Girls* thing, 'Posh Girls by the Seaside', I don't know. She was only 15, OK? Don't judge her. Obviously his plan was to trap her into marrying him. They'd already got as far as Ramsgate by the time I cottoned on. I'd appreciate you not mentioning it to anyone as obviously it would be ruinous for her. I've already managed to destroy most of the preliminary sketches. She has told the story anonymously in a ladies' periodical, which I attach here and hope you will not find too scandalous for your fine eyes.

As to your sister and Charles Bingley, I'm afraid I was of the very strong opinion that she just wasn't that into him. Did I get that wrong? 'My bad', as I think they say in Cheapside? Also, I meant what I said about your family. You and Jane are lovely, but you do come with . . . baggage. So yes, I did say she wasn't into him and he should move on. Thought it was kindest in the end, given that he kind of needs a devoted wife with a good family – he's not got the most cop-on as you've seen. I am terribly sorry if I was wrong about Jane's feelings, though.

I hope this sets things straight between us, and I'm very sorry for the mix-up about Jane – you have to admit her countenance is serene in the extreme, though.

Anyway, I hope your family is well.

Best wishes for your health and happiness.

Regards to your family,

D

P.S. Your dad isn't a tradesman, is he?

17 April 1812

Lizzy
Hope all ok in London. Forwarding
you an email xxx

Regency Teen

Your Problems
Ruined by a rake? Only allowed to go to
Eastbourne, not Brighton? Engaged to your
cousin since your cradle? We've got you covered

Unwed at 18?
Why you still have time

'I was targeted by a fortune hunter'
One brave heiress shares her story

32 ways with bonnets

Swoon!
your favourite redcoats without their red coats

Get a move on!
when your older sister has not the means or
inclination to marry

Top ten seaside towns for a scandalous elopement!
we've all been there: you're a teenager sick to
death of chaperones and older siblings, and you
just want to run off with a penniless rake. Here's
our list of the top seaside towns in which to ruin
yourself!

Ramsgate
Brighton
Lyme Regis
(Read more)

Lady Catherine de Bourgh
@herladyship
Bio: One of the most cultured ladies in England, with the finest taste in music. Britain's most skilled pianist (should I have ever learned). Mother, aunt, landowner, hostess. I must have my share in the online conversation!

Lady Catherine de Bourgh
@herladyship
17 April 1812, 3am

It has come to my attention that some young ladies have no idea at all how to properly pack their gowns in a trunk. None. At. All. Just let that sink in. So buckle up everyone, it's time for some GOWN THEORY. THREAD (1/874)

 @marialikecareylucas Oh God

18 April 1812

 **Lizzy Bennet** Sad to be leaving Kent soon, although a lot has happened, so . . .

 Lady Catherine de Bourgh You seem very out of spirits at the thought of leaving, Miss Bennet. Why not stay on? I'll even take you to London myself if you stay a month

 William Collins Such benevolence!

 Lady Catherine de Bourgh Yes well, can't stand the idea of two young girls travelling alone on the Post! Without a chaperone! Most improper. I was very careful to send someone with my dear niece Georgiana last summer so she didn't get into any trouble.

 Lizzy Bennet My uncle will send a servant for us when we take the MegaPost

Lady Catherine de Bourgh Hmph. Well. Someone must think of these things. Use the code 'QUITE PUT OUT' to get 10 per cent off at the snack bar – they know me there

 Lizzy Bennet Thanks

Lady Catherine de Bourgh It's all extremely vexing, though. I hope you at least watched my ThouTube guide on how to pack a trunk

 Maria Lucas I did! I watched it 14 times!

18 April 1812

Jane
OMG that email!

> **Lizzy**
> I know right?

My head just exploded. Poor Mr
Darcy! You turning him down, and
then having to tell you all that.

> Have to say it looks like Mr D is not
> the addlepate here.

Poor Mr Wickham!

> Come on Jane, there's no way we
> can make both of them good. God,
> can't believe I've been such an idiot
> over Wickham. Totally bought into
> that whole zen yoga vibe. Come to
> think of it, it was pretty odd that he
> told me all that stuff so quickly.
> Plus, how is it zen to join the army?

Looked like you cut off the last few
lines of the email though, did I miss
something else in there?

Oh, ha, no. Just some random chat about footpaths. Nothing else. Didn't want to bore you with it

So you didn't find anything out about Mr Bingley huh?

Working on it . . . What should I do about Wickham though? If it's true, shouldn't we warn people?

Hmm don't think we should tell anyone. Just in case. Also not fair on Georgiana to expose her like that! And maybe Wickham is reformed now. Plus I think that heiress dumped him so he's probably trying to make his way again. Everyone deserves a second chance.

Yeah you're right. Ha, I mean what are the odds of him trying something like that again?

11 May 1812

The Hertfordshire Militia
The regiment is excited to announce it will be holidaying in sunny Brighton this summer!

 Lydia Bennet Oooooooh. All the officers and a whole camp-ful of soldiers. **Mrs Bennet Mr Bennet** it's cool if I go right?

 Lizzy Bennet Definitely not! Dad, you'd better not say yes or I swear

 Mrs Bennet Don't forget your cossie! A little sea bathing will set you up for life

 Mr Bennet Hmmmm let me think . . .

 Lydia Bennet Pleeeeeeease Dad. Pls pls pls pls pls pls pleeeeeease. Pls

 Mr Bennet Absolutely not.

 Mrs Forster Actually, I could really do with a pal down there Lyds! Why not come and stay with us?

 Mr Bennet Oh fine, as long as I don't have to pay

 Lizzy Bennet DAD!

 Kitty Bennet WHAT. THE. ACTUAL? What about me??? I'm two years older???

11 May 1812

> **Lizzy**
> Just think this is a really bad idea Dad.
> There's some stuff you don't know. People
> she's . . . offended. Plus I really don't think all
> those soldiers are above board!

Mr Bennet
She'll be fine! I'll drop the Colonel a text,
tell him to look out for her. And look, she
gets a free holiday and we don't have to
pay for her to be at Club Med or whatever. What stuff anyway? What people?

> Doesn't matter

She won't stop going on about it.
We might as well let her get it out
of her system

> Not everything is about having an
> easier life, you know, Dad

I promise you get to say 'I told you so' if this
all goes terribly wrong, haha. Just forget
about it and enjoy your trip to Derbyshire
with your Aunt and Uncle Gardiner! Spare a
thought for your poor old dad stuck at home
with your mother and Mary and Kitty . . .

Lydia Bennet @lydiabennet

19 MAY 1812

Woohoo, off to Brighton, don't wait up for me! ;)

@kittybennet I will never get over this

Mrs Gardiner @mrsgardiner

21 JULY 1812

Excited to be taking my dear niece **@lizzybennet** to visit the best of all counties – that's right, it's Derbyshire! Come on you Rams! I think it the greatest place in the world – and I should know, I used to live there! Derbyshire! I should be happy to stay my whole life in Derbyshire.

Get 25 per cent off dinner with a three-night stay NOW at the Lambton Inn (link in bio) #VisitDerbyshire #BestOfAllCounties #AD #paidpartnership #spon

25 July 1812

Mr Gardiner
Look, it's definitely jam then cream, not having this debate again

Mrs Gardiner
Pemberley tomorrow? I know you're not a fan of the owner, Lizzy, but Wickham spent his childhood there so it can't all be bad!

Lizzy
Ughh dunno. Bit over looking at other people's amazing houses tbh. Starting to think the French Revolutionaries had a point!

Lizzy
Sorry that was just a joke obvs it was awful #neverforget

Mrs Gardiner
Oh come on, you've gotta be curious to see how Darcy arranges his sock drawer

Lizzy
What if he's there??!

Mr Gardiner
Checked, they're all away. I'm in! Hope they have a gift shop

Mrs Gardiner @mrsgardiner

26 JULY 1812

✈ Pemberley

So excited to visit beautiful Pemberley with my niece
@lizzybennet today! Looking forward to a ramble in
those extensive grounds . . .

@charlottelucas_collins Oh wow, it's meant to be huge
isn't it!! #sizematters

@georgianadarcy Oh such a shame we're not there yet,
would be great to meet Lizzy and her family! Heard lots
from my big bro. On our way though!

@lizzybennet Wait what?

AskJane

Logged in: Lizzy Bennet

SEARCH HISTORY

How much is Pemberley worth

How many billiard rooms does Pemberley have

Help discovered in a man's house plausible excuses

26 July 1812

Fitzwilliam
EMERGENCY, Charles, help please

Charles
One sec, just trouncing the footman at piquet

I am having a situation

Returned a bit earlier than everyone else,
and Lizzy Bennet is HERE. AT MY HOUSE.
She saw me in my shirt! MY SHIRT,
BINGLEY. Jumped in the lake, didn't I, like
some kind of wild-swimming twat

Ahahahhaaaaa

This is serious

🌢

What is that? What are you doing?

🌢

Because of the swimming? I don't
understand

26 July 1812

> **Lizzy**
> EMERGENCY JANE HALLLLLP
> PLEASE

Jane
Hang on, just stringing up some
herbs

> Jane HE IS HERE

Where r u?

> PEMBERLEY

> That's right, his HOUSE. Not my
> idea, but we were promised he
> wasn't home!!

Oh God. Awks

> I saw him IN HIS SHIRT

. . . and?

Oh God he's really hot. Must be all that fencing. Shirt was quite . . . see-through

Now he's being really weird and nice to Aunt and Uncle G, not snobby at all, what on earth? Invited us to dinner even (appaz the Bingleys are about to descend, sorry babe, but will do a little digging). What's going on? Personality transplant??

Well

You better not say anything about the plague or so help me

26 July 1812

Mrs Gardiner
Look, Lizzy, just did a quick four-hour deep dive on Mr Darcy and found all these, hardly the proud Darcy you spoke of??

Mrs Jenkins
Huge thanks to my master **Mr Darcy** who surprised me with a new apron for Michaelmas day! #gentlemandonegood

Bob Tenant
Three cheers for our master **Mr Darcy** who has never put us out on the streets to starve! And never beaten anyone! What a prince he is

Georgiana Darcy
My brother is sooooo good to me, look at this new pianoforte he got me! ♥♪

Lizzy
Jesus, you should work for the Bow Street Runners, Aunt

Weird given all the awful stuff he did to dear Wickham isn't it?

I dunno, I'm starting to wonder if we got that right

Well something's definitely up, this isn't the Darcy you described at all. He's taking your uncle G fishing tomorrow!

Am I The Addlepate?
AITA for changing my mind after seeing his massive . . . erm . . . grounds?

Posted by /excellentwalker 27 July 1812

I (F, not yet 1 and 20) have known this guy (28M) for a while. We didn't exactly hit it off at first – he was really rude. Wouldn't dance at a ball where gentlemen were scarce – kind of extreme things like that. Plus I heard some pretty bad stuff about him. Anyway a few months ago he proposed, took me totally by surprise and obviously I said no.

Thing is, I've since found out a bunch of things, including that the bad stuff I thought I knew about him wasn't true (that's another story!). I'm really starting to think I might have got him wrong. He's being so nice to my decidedly-beneath-him relatives, and all his tenants seem to love him. Feel like I made a big mistake.

Does it look bad that this is happening right when I just saw his insanely beautiful mansion for the first time though?? What's he going to think of me?! I've always said I wouldn't marry a guy just because he's super rich, but genuinely I'm starting to feel differently about him.

On the other hand, I know he did some bad stuff that has really upset my sister (literal saint, 23F). But the more I think about his reasons (mainly my embarrassing family) I can kind of understand him looking out for his friend. I dunno though, AITA?

I couldn't help but wonder – which is bigger: my feelings for him, or his extensive grounds?

27 July 1812

> **Lizzy**
> Do you think he still likes me?

Jane
Do you care??

> I don't know. He seemed really . . .
> different. Like, actually friendly?
> And everyone here seems to think
> he's some kind of saint or some-
> thing. PLUS he was so nice to Aunt
> and Uncle G, even though they're
> like 50 steps down the social
> ladder.

Are you thinking . . .

> I don't know!! It was just really nice
> to see him. UGH he must think I'm
> a total a-hole. Who goes to see a
> guy's house after they turned him
> down?? Oh hi, just checking out
> the mansion that could have been
> mine, no biggie

So are you gonna see him again?

28 July 1812

Georgiana Darcy
So happy to finally meet **Lizzy Bennet**! Great time at Pemberley with **Fitzwilliam Darcy**, **Caroline Bingley**, **Charles Bingley**, **Louisa Hurst** and **Mr Hurst** plus ace to meet **Mrs Gardiner** and **Mr Gardiner**!

 Lizzy Bennet We really enjoyed it too! xx

*commended by **Fitzwilliam Darcy***

 Fitzwilliam Darcy Wonderful to see you all. Hope you got home safe

 Caroline Bingley Lovely to see you babes. Forgot to ask, are you getting by in Meryton without all the soldiers? I know you were fond of one in particular ;) Must be a terrible loss for your family!

 Fitzwilliam Darcy Caroline, can you just not?

 Caroline Bingley What?!

AskJane

SEARCH HISTORY

Total personality transplant

Q Can you fall for someone you thought you hated?

How to get a man to propose again when you've already told him he's the last man in the world you'd ever marry

28 July 1812

Caroline
You up?

God, so shocked by how EB looked today. That dress must have come from the rag and bone box!

She's grown so brown and coarse, urgh, anyone would think she had to go outside from time to time like some kind of peasant

Her teeth are tolerable I guess, but not out of the common way

Anyway, I'm just starting a new book I brought with me from my extensive collection of many many books. So great to be back at Pemberley and your fabulous library!

Wish I had more space for my books that's all, not much room in a small mansion like Netherfield or the London pad #booksaremyreticule #lovereading #thisgirlreads #bookstagram

Hello? Daarrrrcy talk to meeee

Fitzwilliam
She's the handsomest woman I've
ever met. OK? Hope that clears
everything up for you.

Caroline Bingley
@carolineinthecity
Bio: London and Hertfordshire based. Sister, friend, socialite. Six foot in my head feathers.

Caroline Bingley @carolineinthecity
28 July 1812

If she has:

– inferior connections
– teeth that are tolerable but not out of the common way
– no brilliance in her complexion

She's not the mistress of Pemberley, she's just your side-wench

 **Lydia Bennet** is with **George Wickham**

Surprise beatches! Can't believe we managed to keep this a secret, and you will really LOL when you see me change my profile name to Lydia Wickham! Or Wickham-Bennet? Let me know your thoughts in the comments. Either way, we're out of here, eloping for the win, probably stop in London for a bit. No rush to get wed.

Mrs Bennet, **Kitty Bennet** and 101 others are **Aghast**

 Fitzwilliam Darcy What?

1 August 1812

Mrs Bennet
Lydia my love, this isn't true? One of your pranks like on the ThouTube? You would not have so little compassion for my poor nerves?

Mr Bennet
Kitty, did you know about this?

Kitty
Ummmm

Lizzy
What the hell, Lydia? ELOPED? I have seriously had it with this family

Mrs Bennet
Lydia? LYDIA ANSWER YOUR MOTHER

1 August 1812

> **Lizzy**
> What the actual hell

Jane
I have no idea. They were going to go to Scotland to get married, but now we think they might be in London, doing God knows what

> This makes no sense, she doesn't have any money! Well that's it, it's all ruined, no one will marry us now

Not necessarily. Positive vibes! He might marry her still. He must really love her if he's not in it for any cash . . .

> Huh yeah right. Anyway, that's not what I meant

What did you mean?

> Never mind

1 August 1812

> **Lizzy**
> Hey there, so sorry, we can't make dinner tonight. I guess you've heard . . .

> **Fitzwilliam**
> Yes I heard. Dreadful news. What's being done?

> Dad's gone to London, we're on our way home to help. It's hopeless though isn't it? I mean, we both know what he's like. Please tell Georgiana I'm sorry not to see her

> Sorry, can't talk now. Look after yourself x

> OK. Thanks. I guess see you around.

Meryton Community Discussion Forum
Confined and unvarying since 1653

Warnings of Scams, Frauds and Cads

Posted by **Meryton Cad Awareness Society**
Mr George Wickham has been CANCELLED 7 August 1812

It has come to our attention that a certain young man has been going around with a sob story about how he wasn't allowed to become a vicar by a rich bounder – beware of this, repeat THIS IS A CAD, do not trust him! There is not a tradesman whose daughter has not been meddled with, or who has not been left with an unpaid debt! He has also been known to post under the alias 'NapoleonBonerPart'. For more information please call the Cad Awareness Line – be aware that he might say things like, 'I didn't go to that ball in case scenes should arise,' 'I forbid you to feel sorry for me' or 'Don't be crazy, baby, this tradesman's daughter is simply here to fix the shower.'

Comment /johnlabourer Another tradesman here, hi, yes my daughter meddled with last winter

Comment /bobthatcher Yup, tradesman here can confirm

Comment /mrsvintner Not a tradesman but I know several and they all say yes, daughters meddled with

Comment /keithcheesemonger I'm a tradesman and my daughter hasn't been meddled with so I don't really understand what all the fuss is about

Comment /rogertherake Typical cancel culture. I miss the days when a man could debauch a 16-year-old and receive a pat on the back!

Mrs Bennet Well, here we are. I suppose you've all heard the news about our dearest girl, Lydia, and how she's being meddled with by that cad Wickham – but I always did distrust his appearance of goodness, and I warned the girls! Poor Lydia is so innocent, she probably thought she was going on a coach trip to a museum or something. And now Mr Bennet will fight him and be killed and we shall all be ruined after a certain someone kicks us out of the house! Entail or no entail, it's not right #discrimination. My poor darling Lydia! There have been stories of extravagant debts, intrigues and seductions! Also something about an art project, which doesn't sound at all above board! I ask you all for your kindness and to respect our privacy at this very trying time. Please share this post widely so everyone knows we want to be left alone.

Oh, and if anyone knows a reliable local supplier of smelling salts let me know, no questions asked. Adieu, friends. We are all #ruined.

Mr Gardiner Dear sister, do not give way to useless alarm!

Mrs Philips U no sister I always said he was a wrongun too XXX

Lady Lucas Such a shame, my daughter Charlotte and her clergyman husband were very sorry to hear about this false step, and so was **Lady Catherine de Bourgh**

Kitty Bennet I wish someone would meddle with me

Lizzy Bennet Jesus Kitty, read the room. Mum it's going to be OK, why don't you have a lie-down (and give me your phone)?

www.webapothecary.com

Symptoms

Are you suffering from tremblings, flutterings and spasms in your arms and legs? These are all symptoms of UNWED DAUGHTER disease.

Treatment

Marry off your daughters . . . that's all we've got.

10 August 1812

Kitty
I'm telling you Lyds, the droppings have really hit the spinning jenny over here. Major drama

Lydia
LOL

So . . . are you actually married?

Technically? Not TOTALLY married no. But he is definitely definitely going to get round to it. Tell you what though, I'm really enjoying the meddling, ummmmmm!

Sigh. Well jel

AskJane

Logged in: Lizzy Bennet

SEARCH HISTORY

Q

Has anyone ever married a landowner of some consequence after their sister eloped with a cad?

How to change your name by deed poll

Are wimples itchy

Thoughts from a proud bluestocking

Mary Bennet lives in Hertfordshire and believes a woman's reputation is no less brittle than it is beautiful. She enjoys playing concertos, reading sermons and despairing of her ~~four~~ three sisters.

Brittle and Beautiful: How to be guarded in your behaviour towards the undeserving sex

11 August 1812

Step one: Stem the tide of malice
Step two: Download my new ebook, *The Balm of Sisterly Consolation*, and pour it into each other's wounded bosoms

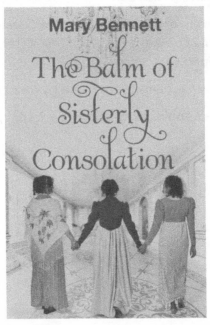

Read more (page 1 of 114)

11 August 1812

Lizzy
I know Mary's a LOT, but she kind of has a point doesn't she?

Jane
Oh Lizzy, you've not been reading her book have you?

No! I just mean about reputations. You know. Being . . . brittle.

We're screwed is what I'm saying

Not necessarily! Perhaps there's been an elaborate and hilarious misunderstanding of some kind

How??? Ugh, can't stop thinking about Darcy. What he must be thinking about me. Telling everyone he was right about my low connections after all. Bet he's thinking he dodged a bullet here

Ummm you turned him down, why do you care what he thinks? #girlpower #ewomancipation. You should read *Looking for Esteem in All the Wrong Estates* and *Gentlemen Are from Eastbourne, Ladies Are from Ramsgate*

12 August 1812

 **William Collins** So sad to hear about the misfortunes of the Bennet family, whose daughter has run away with a cad. Must be even sadder to know it probably arose from your own faulty degree of indulgence. Although I'm a clergyman I'm happy to hold out the hand of friendship to my dear unfortunate cousins – for who else will associate with such a family? Better if she was dead tbh.

 Lizzy Bennet OK then, unfriend us, byeeeee

 William Collins But wait, there's a lot more I have to say

 Lizzy Bennet Too late, unfriending

Am I The Addlepate?
AITA for not caring that my sister made a scandalous alliance?

Posted by kittycatb 15 August 1812

So my (18F) sister (16F) ran off with some hot dude and even though they will get married eventually everyone is losing their minds over it. AITA? I just want a bit of fun too – I'm two years older as well! – but my dad says I can't even go to Eastbourne, let alone Brighton, and no balls unless I dance with my other sisters! WTF?! I will die an old maid, I'm already 18. Surely I am NTA? I just want some fun/to get married unlike my ancient older sisters (23/21 and unwed!!!). And I don't think what my younger sis did was SO bad either. At least she's getting some meddling 😜

TL;DR younger sister eloped so now I have to become a nun basically.

Comment /chaperonesrus Be careful, a woman cannot be too guarded in the presence of gentlemen. Remember the Cad Awareness Line is free to call and if you need a chaperone get in touch, we have maiden aunts on our books for any occasion

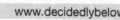
The Support Group for Landowners Drawn to Young Ladies with Low Connections

Posted by derbyshirelad 15 August 1812

Etiquette help needed here, chaps – remember that lady I posted about last year? We've been getting on so well, and I was just about getting used to the idea of aligning myself to her inferior connections, but unfortunately her sister just got 'cad-bombed' as I think you say on here.

Shall I pay him off to marry her? I can just about deal with the total impoverishment, but I think the added scandal of the affair might be a step too far. Thinking of throwing some cash at the problem . . .

Also, in another story, he once tried to marry my own sister – bit awkward at Christmas and everything, you know.

Comment /dontpollutetheshades I regret my marriage to an impoverished young lady, I have been supporting her seven brothers and sisters these 20 years. She never knows what fish knife to use and is always asking whether we really need three billiard rooms #shadespolluted #infamousalliance

Comment /happygolucky Go for it mate – married my tavern wench in 1798 and never looked back. At the end of the day all you need is a warm bosom and a well-pulled pint

Comment /gentlemensrightsactivist Check it's not a scam first – they have lady cads now too you know #iaintsayingshesafortunehunter

PAYCOMPANION
ACCOUNT NAME: **Fitzwilliam Darcy**

16/08	**ALERT:** Mr Wickham has requested 10,000 pounds for: Payment to marry penniless girl whose sister you fancy

05/08	Payment to: Miss Lavinia's School For Dance
	Transaction name: Conversational dance level 1
	Amount: 4 crowns

01/08	Payment to: Regency Gentleman Quarterly
	Transaction name: annual subscription
	Amount: 18 shillings

17 August 1812

Lizzy
Lydia, what the hell is going on?

Mrs Bennet
I cannot cope with this my poor nerves
what a terrible cad to corrupt my poor
innocent lamb like this, I expect I will
die soon with all the stress

Lizzy
Uncle G says you're actually
married now??

Lydia
They wouldn't let me live-stream
the ceremony, losers, but am totes
married!

Jane
Congrats but um . . . how? Will you
be OK?

Lizzy
What will you live off, she means,
you're both penniless, hello

Lydia
Calm down Judgey McJudgerson, Uncle Gardiner paid for everything I guess! He's been a bit grumpy with me but I forgive him

Mrs Bennet
OMG A DAUGHTER WED I LITERALLY COULD NOT BE HAPPIER RIGHT NOW DEAR WICKHAM LOVE HIM SO HANDSOME OMG

17 August 1812

Lizzy
WTF Jane – why would he marry her? She is broke and also quite annoying, and Uncle Gardiner has no money, he lives in Cheapside FFS. Like hello, the clue is in the name

Jane
Perhaps Wickham isn't so bad after all – maybe he was suffering from the plague before

FFS Jane I love you but get a grip

Lydia Bennet @lydiabennetnowmrswickham

31 AUGUST 1812

WEDDING BELLS! He put a ring on it!

So happy to have married my dear dear Wickham. A beautiful day where I got to wed my best friend and soulmate. Nice to see Uncle G, **@mrsgardiner** and **@fitzwilliamdarcy** on the big day too

@fitzwilliamdarcy LYDIA, WHAT DID WE TALK ABOUT?

@lydiabennetnowmrswickham LOL what a lark soz

@mrsbennet You should have waited to talk to me about wedding clothes my love! You do not know the best weddingwear warehouses. You had two weeks in London with dear Wickham, we could have gone shopping!

@lizzybennet Ha ha Mum what are you like, she was only in London the night before the wedding, staying with Aunt and Uncle Gardiner, right Lydia?

@lydiabennetnowmrswickham 😜

31 August 1812

> **Lizzy**
> Aunt G? Why was Mr D at Lydia's wedding pls?

Mrs Gardiner
OK look, you didn't hear it from me but Darcy paid for it all and made your uncle pretend it was him.

> OK my head just exploded

Really? We kind of assumed you knew all about it, given . . . you know

> Given what??

Well, just FYI we both think he's lovely and he's welcome here any time. Guess we should have known all along, he is from #derbyshire after all

> OMG would you stop going on about Derbyshire and explain yourself?

Like you don't already know! Mrs Darcy LOL 😜

Lady Catherine de Bourgh
@herladyship
Bio: One of the most cultured ladies in England, with the finest taste in music. Britain's most skilled pianist (should I have ever learned). Mother, aunt, landowner, hostess. I must have my share in the online conversation!

Lady Catherine de Bourgh
@herladyship
31 August 1812

Most alarmed by report that reached my ears today. Young ladies quitting the sphere all over the place, polluting the shades, eloping scandalously, wall-to-wall infamous alliances. Is this to be borne? It shall not be and here's why.
THREAD (1/870)

RGQ – Regency Gentleman's Quarterly

Today's Top Articles

How to get a flash of her fine eyes

This year's top valets stairs-tested

How to spend it – a new landau or
a sugar plantation in the West Indies?

When you should pay off a rogue to marry her sister

Saucy tavern wenches on benches

1 September 1812

George
Wow, Lizzy, it has been months since our last messages! How've you been?

Lizzy
Fine

Heard you saw Pemberley?

Yep, stayed at Lambton, hung out with the Darcys a bit

Oh right . . . how's Georgiana these days?

Very well! We got on great actually.

Hmm guess she has improved a bit then. Wow you probably drove right through the village where I was supposed to be vicar. I'd love to see it again but I just don't know if I'm emotionally ready for that, you know?

Funny, I heard you weren't very into that plan in the end. Heard all sorts of things actually

You still there?

Sorry, think someone's at the door

Riiiiiight. Tradesman maybe

Let's just put it behind us eh? Guess we are brother and sister now!

Lol not in a kinky way

Unless you're into that ;)

Jesu Christ

Posted by **Mrs Bennet** 1 September 1812

Ladies, won't be leaving the forum any time soon (still four to go, LOL!!!!) but GREAT NEWS one of my IDs is wed and barely 16. One down!! Wait for it . . .

Mrs Wickham.

God, that sounds great.

Thought I'd share how we did it. Full disclosure – this is kind of an extreme method but IT WORKS. First up – you have to not be afraid of a little scandal . . .

Lizzy Bennet
@pertopinionsfineeyes
Bio: Second of five daughters.
Likes walking, winking and
witticisms. She/Her

Lizzy Bennet @pertopinionsfineeyes
3 September 1812

Stuff my parents say
Dad: Into one house they shall never be
admitted!
literally the next day They arrive at our
house

7 September 1812

Lydia
Hi guys, adding my dearest
Georgie Porgie to the group chat!!

Lydia
Have changed the name of the
group too

Lydia
Also removed your admin rights
Jane, you must go lower now I'm a
married woman ;)

Lydia
Anyway was just popping in to let
you know! You probably won't hear
from me loads now, we married
women don't really have time for
chatting!! Byeeee

9 September 1812

Lydia Wickham-Bennet
Byeeee guys, off to Newcastle to join the regiment!! Can't wait to see the soldiers and make some new mates. Lol where even is Newcastle?? Look us up if you're there!

Mrs Bennet Newcastle?!! Surely that's WEEKS away?!

Kitty Bennet VisageTime me?

Lydia Wickham-Bennet Sure! Might be a while though, we married woman don't have much time for the socials

George Wickham Au revoir, adieu, dear friends, I bid you all the fondest of goodbyes *flourishing bow*

John Shopkeep Omg was that French? Reporting this

Jill Washerwoman I knew it, always thought he had a continental air about him

Charles Bingley has checked in to **Netherfield Park** ✈

Guess who's back!!
Back again
Bingley's back
Tell a friend
Lolololoolll

Back for some quality shooting for a few weeks, just love the country!!
Love the city too! #lovemylife!!

(private estate, we're all being tested for the plague before travelling for those asking, don't worry #staysafe)

15 September 1812

> **Hill**
> Hear your lot are back again,
> Nickers

Nicholls
Oh my days. They're off to town,
they're back from town, and who
the hell has to get everything
ready? That's right, muggins here.
Can't even get langoustines at
such short notice! No time to make
the white soup!

Sarah
Don't know what you're complain-
ing about. Pretty sure I'm going to
have to get the curling irons on
standby, like, yesterday.

19 September 1812

Mrs Bennet
Well of course it means nothing to us that they're back. I haven't even thought about Bingley since last year

Lizzy
Mum you've had the fidgets all day!

Mrs Bennet
You are going to visit him Mr B?

Mr Bennet
Hmmm. You promised if I did that last year he'd marry one of my daughters, what happened to that whole plan? Did he marry one of them?? No. I still have four littering up the place

Mrs Bennet
You have no compassion

Lizzy
We get it Mum

Kitty
GUYS I think he's here!! Like literally on the driveway

Mrs Bennet
WHAT

Mrs Bennet
JANE SORT YOUR HAIR OUT IMMEDIATELY

Mrs Bennet
Maybe think about having some nude etchings ready, just in case? You do have the best figure in five counties, after all!

Jane

Kitty
I am NOT doing the etchings. Oh God that man is with him, what's his name? The handsome douchey one

Lizzy
Umm who???

Kitty
Dunno his name

19 September 1812

Jane
So glad that's over. Now we can just hang out and it'll be chill and the whole 'will-they-won't-they' engagement drama is behind us. Just friends

Lizzy
Sure sure, very friendly, the way he was ogling you over the sugar lumps

Might just go have a quick re-read of *Ladies Who Esteem Too Greatly*

Yep, I'm sure a book will totally fix the THROBBING SEXUAL TENSION

You're one to talk

What?!

 **Jane Bennet** is now common and indifferent acquaintances with **Charles Bingley**

 Lizzy Bennet So common. Much indifferent. Wow.

25 September 1812

Charles
It's been so 🖤 seeing Jane again these last few days. God, I don't know why I ever went away. For some reason I thought she wasn't that into me??

Fitzwilliam
Weird, total mystery I guess

Mate, I think I'm gonna pop the question

Shocker

Do I have your #blessing? 💍 🖤

You don't need it, dumbass

Pleeeeease

Oh just get on with it!

💀😄🖤💜☀️💒👰 , Will you organise the stag do??? PUNCH! WENCHES! GENTLEMEN GENTLEMEN GENTLEMEN

Why am I even friends with you?

26 September 1812

Charles

Heyyy Jane, you free to take a quick tea this morning?

Jane
Yes we're all here! Except Lydia, lol. Actually forget I mentioned Lydia. Not relevant.

I more meant you specifically . . .

Come round any time, I'm breezy!! All of us here, v common and indifferent, no worries. Super chill

26 September 1812

Mrs Bennet
😉

Mrs Bennet
😉

Mrs Bennet
😉

Mrs Bennet
😉

Mrs Bennet
😉

Mrs Bennet
😉 @Kitty

Kitty
Mum, what are you trying to say?
Did you sit on your phone again?

Mrs Bennet
😉

Kitty
Is it . . . is it art?

Mrs Bennet
For heaven's sake Kitty stop corset-blocking and leave the room so Jane can get engaged. I'm in the coat cupboard.

Kitty
What are you doing in the coat cupboard?

Mrs Bennet
JUST GET OUT OF THERE

Lydia
Guys can you stop all these messages, really busy being married and don't have time for endless drama OK?

26 September 1812

> **Lizzy**
> GOD SO SORRY Mum literally dragged me out, so awks, shall I come back in? Am outside door.

Jane
Yes please come quick arrgh have never been alone in room with man before! What happens, do we just sit on chairs like normal?

Wait no don't come in

ARGH

Actually yes. Oh God gonna 🤮

> Hang on Mum's spotted me

> Apparently am needed urgently, the langoustines have escaped 😧

Seriously?

> Brb

26 September 1812

Hill
OMG major scenes today. Right in the middle of gutting a fish and what do I have to do, run in and out getting Miss Lizzy away so your master can pop the question, bloody useless aristos

Nicholls
Oh great, guess who'll have to make the white soup for the engagement party, that's right, muggins. Where am I going to get 475 cupcake wrappers at this notice?

Charles Bingley @abingleybingbong

26 SEPTEMBER 1812

She said yes!! We're so happy to announce our engagement #blessed #allswellthatendswell #SPON Thank you to Pompadour Diamonds Inc!

@mrsphilips Congrats Mrs B!! Lots of luv xxx

@mrsphilips I mean, congrats Jane and Chaz!

@mrbennet Congratulations! I know you'll be very happy together. You're exactly the same after all. So chilled you'll never agree on anything, and so generous you'll probably exceed your income! ;)

@mrsbennet LOL Mr Bennet ur so funny, as if dearest Charles would ever run short, not that we even thought about the fact that he has 5k a year, just pleased he and our sweetest girl are so happy! Am sure **@LadyLucas** will also be thrilled for us

@carolinebingley Oh wow. Congrats Chaz on your new in-laws!!

@janebennet Thank you Caroline babes, so pleased we are going to be sisters! **@lizzybennet** you next?! ;)

> **@lizzybennet** Haha, hardly. Thinking of getting some cats and taking up embroidery . . .

> **@fitzwilliamdarcy** 😔

Lizzy Bennet
@pertopinionsfineeyes
Bio: Second of five daughters.
Likes walking, winking and
witticisms. She/Her

Lizzy Bennet @pertopinionsfineeyes
5 October 1812

Check out my sister's ebook guide to
marrying up – **Feel the Sphere and Quit It
Anyway!** #quitthesphere #justforlaughs

 @socialclimber Love this!! I #quitthesphere
ten years ago, went from housemaid to lower-
middle-class merchant's wife, never looked
back! Don't even have to share my bathwater
anymore!

 @herladyship Young ladies and gentlemen of
the nobility should not marry beyond their
own first cousins, this is a very sad state of
affairs indeed Miss Elizabeth Bennet. I AM
VERY PUT OUT

10 October 1812

@herladyship
A report of an alarming nature
reached me two days ago

@pertopinionsfineeyes
Hi Lady Catherine, how are you?
Nice to hear from you as well . . .

@herladyship
After your sister's most
advantageous sphere-quitting

@pertopinionsfineeyes
Look, she didn't actually quit any
sphere, that's just a marketing
thing. We are the daughters of a
gentleman you know! 🙄

@herladyship
ERR your aunts?? Your uncles??
Your slutty sister? I know it all,
missy. So you better not be
thinking of any sphere-quitting
yourself, esp not with my nephew
Mr Darcy

@pertopinionsfineeyes
WHAT? Who's been saying that?

@herladyship
And I suppose this lady is your mother **www.mumsofunwed-daughters.net/MrsBennet**? Obstinate, headstrong girl, I'm ashamed of you!

@pertopinionsfineeyes
Sorry new Witter account who dis?

12 October 1812

Fitzwilliam
Right, so what are we going to do for this 'stag do' then? He insisted on the group name of course

Charles
As long as we have some wenches!!! Only joking, I am very respectful of women #ally #heforshe

Fitzwilliam
It will all be very tasteful – some shooting and the white soup MAY be served by wenches but only high-class ones

Colonel Fitzwilliam
Guys, if you want some new sunnies for the stag do I have a great deal for you **www.shadesof-pemberley.com**

Fitzwilliam
Everyone owes three guineas, make sure to pay before the 21st PLEASE

Sir William Lucas
CAPITAL. Have we considered a trip to St James's Court? Excellent wenches there

William Collins
Thanks for inviting me guys, don't worry, I'm not a regular vicar I'm a fun vicar! Don't mind the odd wench as long as I can read to her from Fordyce's Sermons

Mr Hurst
Will there be any port pong?

12 October 1812

Lizzy
Right ladies, let's have some exciting ideas for our dear Jane's hen do! So far we have:
Bonnet-making workshop
Pin the tail on the Frenchman
'Indeed I have not' drinking game

Caroline
Oh cute, for Louisa's hen do we went to Luxembourg, just saying. Only took four days to get there. Maybe an idea. We must all pay for Jane of course!

Jane
Oh no need! You are so sweet!

Louisa
I'm gluten intolerant, will there be gluten-free cupcakes?

Charlotte
How about a trip to Ramsgate?
Very easy for me now I'm preggers

Lizzy
NO TO RAMSGATE

Georgiana
So happy!!!! Have never been to a hen do before. As long as we don't go near Ramsgate

Kitty
Oh I was hoping for a seaside town of some kind, so that I might expose myself in a public place

Mary
Ugh society has claims on us all I suppose. I'm in, so long as I can have my mornings to myself for some sober reflection

Lydia
Soz can't make it, too busy being married

Maria
Awesome, party time! Will make sure my gowns are all packed right

Mrs Gardiner
I know where we can go!

Lizzy
Don't you dare say Derbyshire

Mrs Bennet
As long as I have a good supply of smelling salts for my poor nerves! What about some Redcoats in the Buff to serve us claret?

Lizzy
MUM

16 October 1812

Fitzwilliam
Good day, Miss Bennet. Hope you
are still amenable to walking towards
Meryton today? It is a fine day

Lizzy
Sure! We're all going though aren't
we?

Jane and Bingley, you and me

Oh and Kitty wants to come

Oh. Great.

OK listen. I literally can't deal with
not saying it, I know about the
paycompanion

Oh God listen, that was just one time
for research, I wanted to see if dirty-
petticoat erotica was a real thing

I mean the payment for Lydia's
marriage? What are you talking
about?

. . . nothing

Well, OK, thank you anyway, it was really kind of you. Especially given all that business with Wickham

No biggie

Well it kind of is a biggie. Thank you and that goes for my family too. They don't know obvs but they would be so grateful if they did

Well, much as I respect your family I think I only did it for you

Oh

Look if you still want me to 'get in the sea' . . .

OMG no! I mean, I was wrong. I'm sorry for all that stuff I said.

Me too. Not my finest hour. My affections and wishes are unchanged though.

So mine are . . . kind of different now . . .

Will you be wearing petticoats today out of interest?

????

Maybe it's going to be a bit muddy

Sorry, never mind

16 October 1812

Kitty
Well this is nice and awkward, out for a walk with my sisters, my sister's fiancé and some dude who clearly fancies my other sister and me just stuck at the back while Mr Darcy awkwardly talks to Lizzy about the mud

Kitty
I'm off up the lane to see Maria, this is way too 'fifth wheel' for me

Lizzy
Kitty, don't leave me with him

Lizzy
Actually, yes do

Lizzy
Argh!

Mrs Bennet
KITTY, GET IN THE COAT
CUPBOARD

Kitty
Mum we are outside

17 October 1812

Mr Bennet
Oh Lizzy, my love, are you sure about this? I mean, you've seen what happens when husbands and wives don't get on . . .

All I'm saying is, you don't have to do this just because of money. I know you'll be out on the street when I pop my clogs but don't worry, I'm planning to take up Zumba any day now

Lizzy
Oh Dad you old softie. I promise I'm not, ok? I really love him. He's actually the most amazing guy. Just takes a while to get to know him, that's all.

And there I thought you hated him! When did this happen?

Hard to say, it happened so gradually. I mean, seeing Pemberley didn't hurt ;)

Oh stop it

Fitzwilliam Darcy married Lizzy Bennet

For those who couldn't make it to the wedding (such a shame you were called away for that urgent facial, **Caroline Bingley**!) here's the speech in full:

'So as some of you know, Lizzy and I kind of had a rocky beginning. (Pause for general laughter.) Thanks, **Charles Bingley**, for bringing out that etching I did of her at the Meryton ball by the way, gave us all a good laugh.

Many of you probably don't know that I actually proposed for the first time back in April (pause for general exclamations of astonishment). Let's just say it didn't go all that well. I think her exact words were 'the mode of your declaration just made it easier to say no' – ouch (pause for sympathy).

Anyway, that's all in the past! She seemed to change her mind when she saw my beautiful grounds, ha ha! I ain't saying she's a gold-digger,

but Aunt Catherine certainly is! (Pause for laughs/duck for cover.)
Thanks for coming anyway, Aunty C, despite all that shade-polluting,
and thanks for the gift of the small summer estate.

As for me, I cannot fix on the hour, or the spot, or the look, or the
words that started me off. I was in the middle of being in love before I
knew I had begun. I haven't always been great at saying what I feel, but
I'm here to tell you I feel like the luckiest landowner in Derbyshire.
Second time lucky! Now please raise a glass of port to my wife! Mrs
Darcy! (Pause for claps.)

Oh, and in case anyone was wondering, yes, I will be dancing later!'

15 November 1812

Mrs Bennet A double wedding! Three daughters
married! Such sons-in-law! In your face **Lady
Lucas**! #mrcollinswho #didbetter

Lady Catherine de Bourgh I am very put out

Lizzy Bennet-Darcy
@pertopinionsfineeyes
Bio: Second of five daughters.
Likes walking, winking and
witticisms. She/Her

Lizzy Bennet-Darcy @pertopinionsfineeyes
15 November 1812

*Stuff my parents say (on my wedding day,
lol!)*
Mum: OMG three daughters married! I shall
go distracted!
Dad: If any young men come for Mary or Kitty,
send them in, for I am quite at leisure!

Lizzy Bennet-Darcy
@pertopinionsfineeyes
Bio: Second of five daughters. Likes walking, winking and witticisms. She/Her

---

Lizzy Bennet-Darcy @pertopinionsfineeyes

15 November 1812

How it started/How it's going

Lizzy
LOL – safe to say I will never dance with Mr Darcy!

✓ *commended by **@puttingonthefitz***

Glossary

AITA: Questions of etiquette weigh upon all of us, particularly following a large social engagement or an infamous scandal. If you're wondering if your behaviour has been beyond reproach, do not ponder alone. A kind, welcoming and non-judgemental community of caring and fair minded people awaits you online, to help you decide – Am I The Addlepate?

Capital Relocation: Looking for your first starter mansion? Taking a townhouse in Bath for the summer? In need of a modest country retreat for you and four and twenty house guests? Whatever your requirements, we guarantee you a Capital Relocation!

Commendable Reads: We do declare there is no enjoyment like reading! Share your decided opinions on the literature of the day.
'The Castle of Otranto: hardly any time spent in castle! 1 star, Mr Biggins, Shropshire'
'Tom Jones: A right rollicking romp!! 5 stars, Mistress Pringle, Bishop's Itchington'

Deliveroux: No time to make a roux? Four and twenty diners about to descend upon you? A lady of a delicate constitution in need of a reviving broth? We've got you covered! Our fleet of riders are waiting for your telegram.

Instafootman: When your own footman lets you down, we provide a discreet and efficient service, no questions asked. Fencing lessons available on request.

StringQuartetify: Bring the elegance of a quartet of players into your apartments, without the distress of their unkempt physical presence!

Visage-Time: Are you pining for a friend or family member's visage? Are you confined to your room with a mysterious illness with no immediate prospect of society or amusement? Have you and your sweetheart been parted by scandal, or a case of the pox? Do not despair: upload your etching and share your visage LIVE with visage-time!

Webapothecary: Tremblings and flutterings all over? An ache in your pate caused by a daughter's exuberant spirits? Caught in a perilous light rain shower?* Identify your ailments and calm your nerves with our fulsome directory of the latest medical science! Leeches, smelling salts and dental chisels available for swift despatch.
*Webapothecary cannot condone or encourage ladies to perambulate in any but the most clement of conditions. Please venture forth at your own risk.

Witter: Do you have more opinions of a fervent nature than your acquaintances and kin have the means or inclination to digest? Are you dying to share your thoughts on the apparel or discourse of the moment? Witter on at your leisure with likeminded folk who will provide rapid, ardent and impassioned feedback on your every utterance!

Acknowledgements

Our most profound and ardent thanks . . .

to Sara Adams and Bea Fitzgerald for editorial magic, our cover designer Lydia Blagden, image designer Becky Glibbery, marketer Callie Robertson, publicist Niamh Anderson, text designer Craig Burgess, production controller Claudette Morris, copyeditor Holly Kyte and to everyone else at the brilliant Hodder Studio team and beyond who has helped to bring this project to life and spread the word

to our wonderful agents, Juliet Mushens and Diana Beaumont, for making it happen

to photographer Johnny Ring and everyone who helped with our photo shoot, especially Libby Earland. Huge thanks to our team of fabulous models – all of whom are Hodder & Stoughton staff, or friends of the authors and the Hodder Studio team. Special thanks to our BFF (bosom friend forever) Angela Clarke, who was there at the inception and has listened to many iterations of this over the years (sorry)

to our families and friends, especially those who've shared our love of *Pride and Prejudice*/quoted large sections verbatim with us – and to everyone who shared and commented on our original social media posts in the midst of lockdown

to Andrew Davies for THE adaptation, which has been etched in our brains since it first aired on the BBC in 1995

and, of course, to the incomparable Jane Austen, who would definitely have a Twitter following of millions were she around today.